Unforgettable Soccer

"My idea of paradise is a straight line to the goal."
–Friedrich Nietzsche

"All that I know most surely about morality and obligations I owe to football." –Albert Camus

UNFORGETTABLE

SOCCER

TALES OF THE BIZARRE, INCREDIBLE, AND SPECTACULAR

Meyer & Meyer Sport

British Library Cataloguing in Publication Data
A catalogue record for this book is available from the British Library

Originally published as *Historias insólitas del fútbol.*
Unforgettable Soccer
Maidenhead: Meyer & Meyer Sport (UK) Ltd., 2019
ISBN: 978-1-78255-162-1

© 2019 by Meyer & Meyer Sport (UK) Ltd.
Aachen, Auckland, Beirut, Cairo, Cape Town, Dubai, Hägendorf, Hong Kong, Indianapolis, Manila, New Delhi, Singapore, Sydney, Tehran, Vienna

Member of the World Sports Publishers' Association (WSPA)
Printed by C-M Books, Ann Arbor, MI, USA
ISBN: 978-1-78255-162-1
Email: info@m-m-sports.com
www.thesportspublisher.com

CONTENTS

Contents

Contents

PREFACE

On October 26, 2013, soccer, the most popular and exciting sport in the world, celebrated 150 years. It was on that day in 1863 when a group of visionaries met in a London pub called *Freemason's* to create *The Football Association* and write the first "official" regulation for a new game, thereby setting it on its prestigious path. Since then, the ball has rolled along a vast and profuse road—and through stadiums—all over the world, and in millions of professional and amateur matches.

In popular memory, the great champions, the stars, and the gigantic feats are remembered. But these moments are not the focus of *Most Incredible Soccer Matches*. To write this book, I've dug into the sands of time in search of the most unusual matches, not the most transcendental ones. This book does not intend to recreate facts that have an important place in the history of soccer, but rather to recollect spectacular events that also deserve a place—though modest perhaps—for their unforgettable and unique characteristics. Many great clubs and players will be mentioned, as well as anonymous soccer players or unknown teams, because unexpected, curious, funny, and memorable episodes happened to them.

I'll give you a few examples: a soccer player who scored all four goals of a game that ended 2-2. One referee who stopped the game to find the false teeth he had lost, another who sent off a coach when he learned that he was a "friend" of his wife, and a third who was about to be run over by the car of a player furious by the punishment he received. A goal scored by a dog and another by a seagull. A team thrashed after using a one-armed goalkeeper and another because their players had arrived having imbibed several more drinks than they should have during a player's marriage ceremony. A midfielder who ate the referee's red card and a defender who was suspended for a match even though, at the time of the ruling, he had been dead for more than a week. A match that had to be canceled due to the appearance of an iceberg and one striker who was sent off twice...in the same game!

These are just some of the extraordinary stories found in *Most Incredible Soccer Matches*. One note: In this book you will find very few references to the World Cups, the Champions League, or the Olympic Games, since these competitions have their privileged space in my other books. Some circumstances that occurred in those contests were cited to serve as a context for other curiosities; however, it's not the renown of the tournaments that make up the soul of this book, but the magical rebounds of the ball, regardless of field, rivalry, or country. I invite you to continue reading and enter an amazing but real world. Welcome to the most incredible soccer matches!

–*Luciano Wernicke*

THE WEDDING

The return leg against AFC Comprest GIM meant a double commitment for the players of CS Viitorul Chirnogi. On the one hand, they had a sporting commitment to face the second division of Romania in the second match of the promotion league after a shameful 0-10 in their first match. On the other hand, they had the human commitment: One of the starting players was getting married the night before the defining match. Another player proposed to assume both responsibilities, so they all approved, even knowing that a wedding was not the best place to concentrate before the match. On the morning of June 20, 1993, all of Viitorul Chirnogi's players showed up for the match drunk after so many toasts to the health of the new couple. Their performance, funnily, provoked a "double" result, much like their blurred vision: 21 to 0 for the fresh and sober athletes of Comprest. And it was only 21 because the referee ended the match in the 70th minute when only six of the drunken players were still standing.

GOLDEN GOAL

When a match is defined in an "all-or-nothing duel," it tends to run longer than it should. And while the teams change sides, there is no time for anything. In April of 2000, Surnadal Idrettslag (of the Third Division) and Sunndal Fotball (of Second Division) did not put a dent on the scoreboard at the Syltøran stadium where they faced each other in a match for the Norwegian Football Cup. After 90 minutes and the first 15 minutes of extra time, the score remained 0-0. In this nerve-wracking atmosphere, the goalkeeper for the host team, Olav Fiske, unable to run all the way to the locker room, proceeded to relieve some of that "tension" behind his goal. But the ref did not notice this and blew the whistle to have the play resume, with Sunndal playing the ball from the middle of the pitch. The seasoned midfielder Oddvar Torve noticed that Fiske was still behind the goal and took advantage of it: He kicked the ball directly from the center circle, and it went meekly into the goal. "This situation caused me great shame," said the humble goalkeeper to the press after the match. Sunndal advanced to the next round, and the Surnadal officials demanded the match be cancelled and then rescheduled, not because of the goalkeeper's mistake, but because they believed that the referee authorized the restart without realizing that Fiske was not prepared. Their complaint was dismissed by the Scandinavian Federation, which took as legitimate a goal that was truly "golden."

THE BAG'S GOAL

On May 27, 1934, during the derby between CA Peñarol and Nacional Football Club played in the Centenario stadium of Montevideo, one of the most unprecedented cases in Uruguayan soccer took place. Amid an attack by the Peñarol team, Brazilian striker Bahia took a violent shot to the goal of the tricolored Nacional team, which ended up going out by end line. But the ball bounced against the bag of one of the physical trainers, who was watching the play from behind the end line, and returned to the field. Another Peñarol striker, Braulio Castro, took advantage of Nacional's relaxed defense and sent the ball into the back of the net. The referee Telésforo Rodríguez, who hadn't noticed the strange situation, validated the goal. Angered by ref's decision, the eleven National players rushed him and gave him a ferocious beating. Because of this, the derby had to be suspended.

THE PENALTY SPOT

The talented Scottish leftie Archie Gemmill was having a lovely afternoon in the Baseball Ground, the former stadium of Derby County FC. That rainy afternoon of April 30, 1977, the club from the heart of England was beating Manchester City FC 3-0, and none of the visiting players could stop the skilled Gemmill. At least legally because, with four minutes left, midfielder Gary Owen fouled him inside the penalty area right after a corner kick, resulting in a penalty kick. Gerry Daly, midfielder for the host team, took the ball and looked for the spot to place it, but the penalty mark had disappeared in the mud. The witty Manchester City goalie Joe Corrigan tried to convince the ref to place the ball almost on the edge of the penalty area, to which he received a yellow card for his efforts. As the search proved unsuccessful, the referee called the stadium steward, Bob Smith, who came armed with a tape measure, a paintbrush, and a bucket of white paint. After stretching the tape 12 yards, Smith took the brush and drew a circle on the wet ground. Daly put the ball on the wet paint, took a running approach, and kicked a right cross shot Corrigan was unable to stop. A goal "tailored" to close the victory 4-0.

THE URN

The strong security guard at the Benito Villamarín stadium in Seville stood firm: "He cannot enter with that." "But," replied the young green-and-white fan, "I have his annual pass here!" The guard took a few seconds to recover from his surprise, but stood firm: "Even if he has a pass, it's dangerous, it's forbidden to enter with a blunt object, if you or anyone throws it to the field or to another section of the grandstand, it can cause serious damage." "How am I going to throw a funeral urn into the field?" the boy asked himself, disappointed and anguished by the refusal. But, immediately, a brilliant idea occurred to him. He went to a nearby supermarket, bought a carton of milk, emptied it in the lane of the sidewalk and, with borrowed scissors, improvised a container for his father, or rather, the ashes of his father, that would be allowed. On his deathbed, the man had asked his son to continue attending matches so he could "see" his beloved Real Betis Balompié after dying from a serious illness. Thus, in a container of harmless cardboard and with his ticket for the 1995/96 season, the deceased entered the Andalusian stadium with his obedient son to enjoy the first home game of the season, a 3-1 victory over Real Zaragoza SAD.

THREE FOR THE PRICE OF ONE

Can three different players miss the same penalty? Of course! There seems to be no limit to the list of soccer curiosities. On September 22, 1973, Portsmouth FC received Notts County FC in Fratton Park for the English Second Division Championship. The visiting club had the opportunity to open the scoring by a penalty shot, but the scoreboard remained blank since the shot was missed by Kevin Randall, Don Masson, and Brian Stubbs. How was this possible? Randall's shot was saved by local goalkeeper John Milkins, but the referee ordered it to be retaken because the goalkeeper had stepped ahead of the line. Randall did not want to face the situation again and left his place to Masson, who scored, although the goal was invalidated because the referee had not given the order to kick. Upset, Masson gave his chance to Stubbs, who waited for the whistle, took a run, kicked...and missed the goal. The unsuccessful trio was immortalized by this show of lack of skill, but, at least that afternoon, they went home to Nottingham victorious, with a 1-2 score, thanks to the goals scored by two of their more talented companions, Arthur Mann and Les Bradd.

THREE RED CARDS IN FOUR DAYS

Can anyone match the record of the clumsy Albanian defender Agim Shabani? This defender for the Norwegian club Fredrikstad FK was sent off for repeated fouls on June 24, 2007, the day on which his club fell as visitors 2-1 against Strømsgodset IF for the Norwegian Premier League. The next day, Shabani—just 19 years old—was summoned to play a reserve game. The man could not help himself and again saw the red card for lashing out a few kicks to the opposing players. On the 27th, 48 hours later, the young defender returned to wear the white shirt of Fredrikstad FK against Nybergsund IL-Trysil for the Norwegian Cup. That day, the whole stadium was paying attention to the performance of the Albanian, and he did not disappoint: Shabani was red carded again, and his team fell 1-2. If this man does not appear in the *Guinness Book of World Records,* it is because nobody thought to report this fantastic "feat" of three red cards in four days.

THE TRICK

In 1978, the Cali Sports Association of Colombia achieved an unprecedented milestone for their country: reaching the final of the Copa Libertadores. Led by Argentine Carlos Bilardo, the squad—which had already surprised everyone by reaching the semifinal in 1977—forged an excellent campaign after prevailing in their group stage against their compatriots Club Deportivo Junior of Barranquilla and the Uruguayans Peñarol and Danubio Fútbol clubs.

In the round-robin semifinals, Deportivo Cali was undefeated after playing Alianza Lima of Peru and Cerro Porteño of Paraguay, two very good clubs. But, in the 180 minutes of the two-legged final, "the Greens" could not do much before the greater experience and remarkable efficiency of the Argentine team Boca Juniors. First was a goalless draw in Cali. This was followed by an unquestionable 4-0 in Buenos Aires which gave the "Xeneixe" ("Genoese," as Boca fans and players are called), coached by Juan Carlos Lorenzo, their second consecutive continental title.

In his autobiography *Doctor and Champion,* Bilardo narrated a curious situation that occurred during the second leg in La Bombonera, home of the back-to-back champion: "From that second leg of the final of the Copa Libertadores I was left with something that shows that 'Toto' Lorenzo was a genius, an incredible guy. When we played against Boca at La Bombonera, Diego Umaña, from our team, a specialist in corner kicks, did not make any of them reach the penalty box. When the first half was over, I asked him: 'Diego, what's wrong with you? Why aren't you sending the corner kicks to the penalty box?' 'Mister,' he answered, 'there's a dog that will not let me kick.' 'A police dog?' I inquired. 'Yes. Every time I went to the corner flag, I had him on top, he stuck to me. He wanted to eat my leg! So I couldn't kick well,' he said. A few days later, when I watched the video replay of that game very carefully, I noticed that Umaña had not lied: Every time we had a corner kick in our favor, the policeman who controlled the dog would let go a bit of rope. There was no place to take a run to the ball! Above all, the dog was very fierce, he barked and threatened to bite poor Umaña. Then, I understood why Diego, with good sense, would have chosen to throw bad corner kicks before leaving the field with one leg less. The 'Toto' was very crafty. A genius!"

A STRANGE CHOICE

Shortly before the start of the 1906 first division championship in Argentina, the legendary goalkeeper José Laforia went to Alumni Athletic Club, leaving his former squad, Barracas Athletic Club, without a substitute starter. (Both clubs are now defunct in the soccer universe.) Faced with this emergency situation, Barracas, who did not have another goalkeeper, was forced to try different field players at the goal, but since none of them excelled in that role, the search continued for a new candidate continued daily.

On August 26 of that year, the men from Barracas had to travel to the town of Campana in Buenos Aires—which is located about 32 miles (60 km) north of the City of Buenos Aires—to face the Reformer Athletic Club, a modest group made up of employees from a refrigerator factory. That cold morning, only eight players showed up at the Retiro train station to make the trip to the rival's field. On the way to Campana, the players decided on a revolutionary strategy to counteract the numerical disadvantage: They entrusted the difficult task of guarding the goal to Winston Coe, one of the founding partners of the team, who usually served as defender on the right. But their strategy did not serve them well against the Reformer squad, who won by a resounding victory of 11-0 against the disadvantaged team from Buenos Aires. However, the chronicles of the time—including the newspaper *La Nación*—praised the work of Coe, who was mainly responsible for Barracas not suffering an even more humiliating rout despite one important physical disadvantage…Coe did not have a left arm!

THE MATCH WITH
NO OPPONENT

Hampden Park was overflowing. Newspapers from Glasgow assure us that on April 19, 1879, a day in which the final match of the Scottish Cup between Rangers FC (local institution that had already begun to have a popular fan base though they still had not obtained a title) and Vale of Leven Football & Athletic Club (squad from the city of Alexandria) was played, there was a "never before seen" crowd "inside and outside the stadium."

The 9,000 seats were sold out, and the match had to be delayed for half an hour while the police fought hard to restore order to the spectators in the stands as well as the almost 3,000 fans that were left out on the street. The game began, and the Rangers were very efficient, with a fast goal scored by Willie Struthers. The striker was not finished, though, and, shortly after, scored again against the rival goalkeeper, Robert Parlane, with a powerful shot. But, as goals did not yet have nets at this time, the ball bounced off a spectator in the grandstand and, as quickly as it came out, returned to the field. The play surprised the referee, who did not see how the ball crossed the finish line. He ordered the play to continue, despite protests from the Rangers.

In the second half, Vale of Leven took advantage of a mistake by rival goalkeeper George Gillespie to equalize the score, which remained tied until the end. The Rangers' players and fans were outraged. Their officials protested the result and offered the testimony of the person who had been struck by the uncounted Struthers' goal—a professor of surgery at the University of Glasgow, "a gentleman whose word no Vale fan could doubt." Despite the claim, the Scottish Association maintained the result and ordered the final match to be played again a week later on the same stage. However, on April 26, only one team showed up on the lawn of Hampden Park: Vale of Leven. The Rangers missed the appointment in retaliation against the Scottish Association's decision

At the appointed time, and in the absence of the "blue" players, the referee gave the order and started a ridiculous match of Vale against...nobody! John McDougall, the captain, moved forward and played the ball with James Baird and Peter McGregor until he buried it in the empty goal. The ref—perhaps embarrassed by the unnecessary show—ended the charade, and Alexandria's team lifted the cup for the second time. In the insert added to the base of the trophy, where all the champions are listed, it was written: "Vale of Leven, Rangers did not appear."

FELL FROM THE SKY

A soccer match is an excellent target for advertising campaigns, both commercial and political. The massive competition and the vast variety of spectators make the stadium an important focus for marketing. This was understood perfectly by an intrepid promoter, who, on March 21, 1948, after boarding a plane, flew over the Gemeentelijk Parkstadion where the local team, Koninklijke Boom FC, and Beerschot Antwerpen Club were playing for the first division tournament of Belgium. The pilot, who had loaded the device with advertising flyers, descended, took a package, and threw it through the window to one of the bleachers. The pages dispersed, forming a colorful cloud that caught the attention of the fans, who stretched to grab one of the color papers raining down on them. A major success!

Encouraged by the excellent reception of his strategy, the skilled pilot pointed the nose of his aircraft to the other side of the stadium to repeat the maneuver. But he made an error, and this time, the package did not open and instead fell directly on the head of the referee. In that same moment, Boom FC scored a goal! While the pilot fled, aware that he had made a big mistake, the players and the line judges attended to the referee, who recovered from the knock, luckily, without any major consequences. The referee validated the goal at the request of his collaborators, since he had not seen it, and the game continued as normal. The host club finally lost by 3 to 4, a defeat that seemed to fall straight from the sky.

THE DOG THAT SCORED A GOAL

It is hard to believe this story, although several prestigious English newspapers, such as *The Independent,* swear it is true. In November 1985, the Knave of Clubs FC and Newcastle Town FC faced each other in Monks Neil Park for the Staffordshire Sunday Cup. With the score an unfavorable 0-2, one of Knave of Clubs' defenders sent a ball down the opposite field in attempt to pass to one of his teammates in white. The ball did not reach any of the players, however, because, at that moment, a naughty dog had strolled on to the field. The *dog* ran the ball and, with a nice pirouette, headed it inside the net past a dumbfounded goalkeeper. Then the daring dog fled the field as fast as he could, accompanied by the laughter of the 22 players, the referees, and a handful of spectators.

The laughter did not last long for some of the players, though, because the referee, clearly ignorant of the rules, declared the goal valid. According to the regulations, "in the event that an additional ball, object or animal enters the field of play during the game, the referee shall interrupt the game only if said ball, object or animal interferes in the game." Of little use were the protests of the Newcastle Town's players, especially the goalie, who insisted on telling the ref that he had let the animal do as he wished because such action was not explicit in the law. "Exactly," the referee said, "in the Football Association's regulations, no reference is made to any dog." Faced with the foolish decision of the judge, the ill-treated players of Newcastle decided to return to the game. Despite the referee and the unusual goal, the victims of the dog's antics finally achieved an irrefutable victory, winning 3 to 2.

CONFLICT

When players protest a penalty, they usually get right up in the referee's face—so close that they are practically nose to nose. This scene is so common in matches that when Romanian Remus Danalache protested a bit differently, his method was shared worldwide for its originality.

On October 16, 2011, during a heated match between FC Petrolul Ploieşti and Clubul Sportiv Universitar Voinţa Sibiu in the Romanian First Division, the visiting players wanted to grill the referee Andrei Chivulete alive. They blamed him for their 3-1 partial defeat. They also accused him of unjustly ejecting Claudiu Bunea from the pitch at the 30th minute and goalkeeper Bogdan Miron at the 48th. It was the last straw for the boys from Vointa when, during the 90th minute, Chivulete sanctioned a non-existent penalty for Petrolul. Eight of the players from Vointa protested ardently, going straight into the face of the referee. Substitute goalkeeper Remus Danalache, the ninth remaining player on the field, however, chose to turn his back on the situation…literally. Danalache, who had entered the fray to replace Rares Forika after Miron's red card, decided to protest the ref's performance in a very original way: He faced the shot from the 12-yard spot with his back to the kicker! Consequently, Daniel Oprita, who had already scored twice that afternoon, sent the ball to the back of the net while the goalkeeper remained motionless.

Chivulete, inexplicably, because the goalkeeper was correctly standing on the goal line, invalidated the goal, ordered the shot to be taken again, and warned Danalache with a yellow card. Oprita returned to the penalty spot and converted to put the score 4-1. The goalkeeper remained motionless, although this time he faced the kicker. At the end of the match, Danalache explained to the press that his original position had been agreed on by his teammates and coach, Alexandru Pelici. Impressed by the surprising behavior of the goalkeeper, the Petrolul fans bid farewell to the rival players with applause and cheers. Chivulete, however, received no such acknowledgment. According to the sports newspaper *Gazeta Sporturilor,* the referee was suspended for six months due to several serious errors, including having ordered the repetition of the penalty "back."

A FIERCE STORM

It's happened to all of us, an untimely internal, bothersome cramp that becomes annoying until finally becoming unbearable. When this happens, you can't move, much less play soccer. On April 12, 1999, Fabián Binzugna, goalkeeper for Deportivo Morón, asked the referee Rubén Favale to temporarily suspend the match against CSD Defensa y Justicia for the B Nacional (Argentina's Second Division) because his intestinal cramping was unrelenting. At 25 minutes into the second half, the western club of greater Buenos Aires had already made the three changes allowed, and the nearest toilet was in the locker room, about a hundred yards from the goal of the desperate Binzugna. "If you have to go to the bathroom, we'll wait for you, you are the goalkeeper," explained Favale, sympathetic to the goalkeeper's torment. The game stopped, but not the goalkeeper's feet, which carried him swiftly to the bathroom.

On the way to the locker room, Binzugna was assisted by the team's physical trainer, who helped him remove his gloves and jersey. But the pain wasn't receding. Binzugna then discovered with dread that the three toilets in the locker room were occupied by those who gone off the field minutes before: the defenders Gonzalo Martínez and Luciano Kirokián and striker Fernando Rodríguez—all experiencing similar intestinal cramping.

Upon learning of the urgency of the situation, Rodriguez, the least in trouble, got out of the way for Binzugna, who quickly "got rid" of the problem and returned to the pitch. Feeling better, the goalie explained at the end of the match that his and his teammates' problem had been food poisoning—something they had eaten for lunch had been off. However, there was someone else whose stomach muscles were tested that day—Morón's poor equipment manager had to endure firsthand (really, on his feet) Martinez's discomfort as the defender's relief began several feet before reaching the toilet.

EXCESSIVE CELEBRATION

Perhaps it was an attempt to mimic other South American goalies like Rogerio Ceni, René Higuita, or José Luis Chilavert that led to Hans-Jörg Butt's poor judgment. On April 17, 2004, at the Veltins Arena in Gelsenkirchen, TSV Bayer 04 Leverkusen was ahead of the home team, Fußball-Club Gelsenkirchen-Schalke 04, 1-2, on a new round of the Fußball-Bundesliga, the German top flight. After 75 minutes, referee Jörg Kessler awarded a penalty to the visiting squad, and Butt went running with his head held high straight to the rival's penalty box to take charge of the play. With a high right cross, the goalkeeper beat his opponent Christofer Heimeroth and was euphoric, embracing all his teammates to celebrate the 1-3 score. The arrogant Butt not only lost a lot of time with his celebration, but he celebrated on his own ground, which allowed the local forward Mike Hanke to restart the game with a direct kick from the center spot, which went directly into the unguarded visitor's net. The clumsy Butt could celebrate, at least, that the match ended with his team still victorious.

ACCELERATED COMPLAINT

It is unlikely there was ever a penalty call that was not protested. If the players don't complain, the coaches do. The fans, of course, always complain. But without doubt, the most unparalleled protest was the unusual revenge that a Yugoslav league soccer player attempted to exact from referee Platon Rejinac in 1965. Rejinac had dared to call the maximum penalty possible against Fudbalski Klub Crvena Zvezda Beograd (Red Star of Belgrade) just one minute from the end of the match and with the score tied. While ten of the players surrounded Rejinac to insult the honor of his entire family, the eleventh member of the victimized team left the field through a side door in apparent calm. However, what seemed like cool apathy soon turned into madness: The player got behind the wheel of his car, drove into the stadium, destroying the fence in the process, and began to chase the referee across the field in an attempt to run him over. After a few minutes of astonishing tension, the incensed player was subdued by the police and eventually sentenced to two years in prison for "attempted homicide." Humorously, the soccer association of Yugoslavia only suspended the player for two years.

SOLD OUT

On March 14, 1936, Bradford City AFC and Doncaster Rovers FC were prepared to face each other in the English Second Division. The two teams were on the field, but the game was delayed: One of the line judges hadn't shown up at Valley Parade. The referee in charge of the match tried to find a replacement, but there was no one in the area who would agree to act as an assistant. When the referee announced that the match would be canceled, the visiting player George Flowers—who had traveled as a substitute but had been left off the field, since changes were not authorized at that time—offered to replace the absentee assistant referee. At the end of the game, the Doncaster players weren't too pleased with their partner Flowers. First, because they had lost 3 to 1 without any help from him; second, because they returned home with less money in their pockets than their pal— they had received 1 pound and 10 shillings each for having been defeated, while Flowers was paid a regular lineman's salary for a match of 1 pound, 11 shillings, and 6 pennies.

ADVICE

Many field players have guarded the goal during penalty kicks around the world, having had to replace red-carded or injured goalies. None of these feats received such remarkable help like the save made by the Chilean defender Cristian Álvarez on October 12, 2002. In the middle of a heated match between Universidad Católica and Universidad de Chile, tied 1-1, the referee Carlos Chandía granted a penalty kick for the away team of Universidad de Chile. The goalkeeper, Jonathan Walker, could not defend his goal because he had gotten hurt during a violent clash against his rival, Mauricio Pinilla.

As the Catholic squad had already made the three substitutions allowed, Álvarez put on his gloves to face the designated kicker, Pedro González. Seconds before whistling to authorize the penalty kick, Chandía put his mouth to Álvarez's ear, and said, imprudently, "to your left you should go, go to your left." And so Álvarez did. The defender-turned-goalie dove to that side and saved the shot. The story had a happy ending for Universidad Católica, but not for Chandía. As his inappropriate advice had been captured by the television's microphones that surrounded the pitch, the unusual mishap spread through the media and ignited a national scandal. The following day, the National Association of Professional Soccer determined, after evaluating the case, that, although the referee could not know for sure where González's shot would eventually go, his irresponsibility and his big mouth definitely cost him a match fine.

THE AMBASSADOR'S ASSIST

The Argentine triumph over the Peruvian team in the last game of the Copa América (organized in Lima in 1927) happened with a strange play that should have been canceled by the Uruguayan referee Victorio Gariboni. Before the match—which took place on November 27 at the National Stadium in Lima in front of some 15,000 people—began, the authorities had arranged for the United States ambassador in Peru, Miles Poindexter, to give the "initial kick," a diplomatic formality very common at that time throughout the world and in most sports.

At the appointed time and with the two teams arranged on the pitch, each in its half, Poindexter kicked the ball into the Argentine field toward the visiting players wearing that day a sky-blue shirt crossed by a horizontal white stripe. The ball reached defender Humberto Recanatini's feet, and, without stopping the action, he executed a long kick to Peruvian territory. The striker Manuel "Nolo" Ferreira, who had sprinted to the rival half, dominated the ball and, to the surprise of the host defenders, who did not move a muscle to stop their action, sent a shot into the goal defended by Jorge Pardón. The Peruvian players protested, but the referee Gariboni validated the conquest because he mistakenly assumed that the match had begun with the touch of Poindexter.

FORGETFUL REFS

On May 6, 2009, when Rosenborg Ballklub received Fredrikstad F.K. during the seventh round of the Norwegian First Division, the referee Per Ivar Staberg left the traditional coin used to determine which team takes first in his locker room. Instead of returning to the dressing room and delaying the start of the match, Staberg had an original idea: to invite the two captains, Mikael Dorsin and Hans Erik Ramberg, to play the traditional children's game "rock, paper, scissors" to determine the winner. This proved to be entertaining for the 15,000 spectators, who had fun seeing how Ramberg needed three attempts (in the first two they had both chosen the same option) to win their right to draw first.

Another clueless ref, Oscar Sequeira, had to expel the Paraguayan Celso Ayala of CA River Plate vocally on August 31, 1997, a day in which the "millionaire" team lost at home, 1-3, to CA Rosario Central in the Argentine League. Why? Because he had forgotten his red card in the wardrobe. The Paraguayan defender took it all in stride: "Actually, I did not understand anything; they red-carded me without taking out the red card!" he commented after the game with a smile.

THE UNDECIDED

Regulation authorizes the referee to modify his decision only if he realizes that it is incorrect, or if he deems it necessary, after a suggestion from an assistant referee or the fourth referee, provided he has not resumed the game or finished the match. This provision could be very useful except that it is often abused, and the consequence can be detrimental, as seen during a soccer match in Israel in August 2009.

That day, during the second half of the First Division duel between Maccabi Tel Aviv FC and Bnei Sakhnin FC, referee Assaf Kenan validated a goal from home side Maccabi, scored by the Armenian Ilya Yavruyan, the third for him that day, sealing a 3 to 1 victory. However, seconds later and at the request of one of his assistant referees, Kenan called a foul by a Maccabi player in the play prior to the goal. But, following the host players' vehement protests, including insults, the referee changed his decision again, validated Yavruyan's goal, and ordered the match to be resumed from the center spot.

The new call then ignited the Sakhnin players, who pounced on the referee, who complained, severely and amid threats to withdraw from the field, and demanded the ref remain firm in voiding the goal. The soft Kenan yielded once again to the claims and arranged for the match to continue 2-1 before the bewildered

8,000 spectators who had gathered at Bloomfield Stadium. The scoreboard, though, ended with an unquestionable 3-1 after Sherran Yeini from the host team clinched the match one minute from the end. Was anyone expelled from the field? Kenan has not yet decided...

COMPENSATION

Selhurst Park, London, January 4, 1998. Home team Wimbledon FC takes their corner kick during their match against Wrexham FC for the third round of the FA Cup, tied at 0-0 and already in additional time. Neil Ardley kicks, the ball flies, bounces off Marcus Gayle's head, and ends up in the net. An astonishing win? For the referee, Steve Dunn, no. This referee with bad timing had blown his whistle a moment before, while the ball was in the air, to end the match. The London squad players and their coach, Joe Kinnear, scream at Dunn, eager to get him on the grill with potatoes that night. There was nothing to be done; the judge refused to be dinner and, above all, maintained his decision to close the match with the blank scoreboard—even though he knew he screwed up.

Racecourse Ground, Wrexham, Wales, January 13, 1998. Wrexham FC and Wimbledon FC are again face to face in the "replay" that must decide which of the two advances to the next round of the famous cup. Again Steve Dunn is officiating. The match is again tied, although 2-2. Again, Wimbledon is on the attack. Again, Neal Ardley launches a cross, and again Marcus Gayle heads it straight into the net. Again, there is controversy: One of the line judges raises his flag to mark the supposedly offside position of Gayle. Dunn breaks the "replay:" This time he validates the goal. According to the referee, the English striker— who would wear the jersey of Jamaica at the World Cup in France that same year—was well onside. Now it is the Welsh who want to murder Dunn. Even more so when, seconds from the end, he fails to grant a clear penalty to Alan Kimble, who had kicked down defender Mark McGregor from Wrexham FC inside the area. The final whistle goes, and Wimbledon moves through to another round. On the trip home, Dunn is calm. At the cost of an injustice, justice was done.

IMPROPRIETIES

On November 8, 1972, for the sixth round of the Argentine National Tournament, CA Huracán beat CA Estudiantes of La Plata 2-0 at their home stadium of Parque de los Patricios. The visitors struggled to get one back and, shortly before the end of the first half, they managed to get referee Washington Mateo to call a penalty kick for them as a result of a clear infringement. However, at the request of one of the assistant referees, who had seen that the foul had been several feet back, Mateo changed the shot from the 12 yards to a free kick outside the Huracán's penalty box. The transcendental decision irritated the red-and-white players, who disapproved of the exchange with energetic gestures and vulgar terms aimed at the man in black.

In the middle of the chaos, the referee took out his red card and showed it to the central midfielder Carlos Alberto De Marta, who he thought had hurled at him a clear and rude insult. The match continued and Huracán, with the numerical difference in their favor, stretched their advantage to a 5-1 final. Mateo raised his report, and a week later De Marta was summoned to testify by the Disciplinary Court of the Argentine Football Association. The player went to AFA's home at Viamonte street 1366, appeared before the ruling body, and, a day later, what could have been a harsh punishment only became a fine for one match for "protest of ruling on the field," according to file 6506 filed in the offical records. Why did they apply such a light punishment? The court considered that the midfielder had hardly been able to articulate an insult clearly audible to Mateo, and not only because of the pandemonium that reigned at that moment: De Marta was deaf and unable to speak from birth!

AUDACIOUS

In January 1965, the federation of the Brazilian state of São Paulo suspended referee Albino Zanferrari for fifteen days, due to his performance in the intense derby Santos FC-Botafogo of Futebol e Regatas, won by the visiting squad. "He judged the game with his own personal rules," remarked the court of the federation that studied the case. What terrible mistake had Zanferrari made? Having shown the red to Edson Arantes do Nascimento, the famous "King" Pelé.

AMNESTIES

On October 19, 1996, the Millerntor stadium of FC Sankt Pauli von 1910 witnessed a unique event: Within only a few moments, a player was given a red card, left the field, had the red card rescinded, and returned to play. This extraordinary event happened as a result of referee Jürgen Aust's confusion during the match between the host team and Sport-Club Freiburg of the Fußball-Bundesliga. In the second half, defender Dieter Frey (jersey number 2) committed a strong foul and was reprimanded by Aust. The referee immediately expelled Frey because, according to his notes, the defender had received a yellow in the first half. Exasperated because he did not remember receiving another card, the player ran to the locker room to get rid of his anger with a cold shower. When he was already under water, Frey was called by a trainer's assistant, Volker Finke. One of the line judges had warned the referee that the player cautioned in the initial half had been Martin Spanring (jersey number 5) and not Frey, so Aust reversed the red and stopped play until the expelled player was reinstated. The defender quickly changed back into his uniform and returned to the field, but the amnesty did little to help their team: Freiburg lost 2 to 0.

Another referee who reversed his decision was Juan Carlos Moreno in the match that, in December 1998, CA Ituzaingó and Defensores de Cambaceres played for the C Division of Argentina (fourth tier). Although, his change of mind was for a very different reason. Moreno called a penalty against visiting striker Luis Alberto Monteporzi, who erupted in anger and furiously criticized the decision with strong insults. The ref, harassed by the harshness of the player, put his hand in his pocket and, when extracting his red card, accidentally pulled out some bills that had been in his pocket. With a little help from the wind, the money blew all over the pitch, and the Cambaceres' players (including Monteporzi himself), with great skill, quickly picked it up and returned it to Moreno. Touched by the noble gesture, the referee changed red for yellow. With their eleven men on the field, Defensores won 3-1.

In 1952, before the Copa Libertadores de América and the European Champions Cup were established, a group of Venezuelan businessmen created a club tournament that had a lot of repercussion and a very pretentious name: the "Little World Cup." This championship, which did not have a qualification system, was developed as a round-robin group with selected clubs from Europe and America, such as Real Madrid CF, FC Barcelona, AS Roma, Sport Lisboa e Benfica, CA River Plate, Botafogo de Futebol e Regatas, São Paulo FC, and Club de Regatas Vasco da Gama. The tournament lasted for eleven years, until 1963. That year, while the Cup was being played, a local guerrilla group called "Armed Forces of National Liberation" kidnapped none other than Real Madrid's top star, Alfredo di Stéfano. The player remained in captivity for 72 hours and, although he was very well treated, and his life was never at risk, the episode scared the foreign teams, and they refused to return.

The first edition of the "Little World Cup," though, saw Di Stéfano as a great protagonist, although not as a member of "the whites" but of Millonarios FC of Colombia, his first team outside of Argentina. On July 27, 1952, Millonarios—which was dubbed "the Blue Ballet" due to the quality of their players and the color of their jerseys—faced, coincidentally, Real Madrid in the stadium of the local club, Universitario de Caracas. The match offered the public a fantastic show of great technical, albeit a little rough, play. One of those tough episodes was led by Di Stéfano and the Galician striker Manuel Fernández Fernández, known as "Pahiño." The two players got into a fistfight in the middle of the field. (An interesting note: A year later, the Argentine would reach Real Madrid and would oust Pahiño who, without a place on the first team, would emigrate to Deportivo La Coruña.) The Venezuelan referee, Rubén Sainz, expelled the two fighters, but neither of them wanted to leave the field. Their refusal and the lack of red cards, which were not invented until a decade and a half later, led to a spirited discussion that lasted for 15 minutes until Sainz got fed up and ordered the match to continue with its 22 original protagonists. The duel ended 1-1 and, serendipitously, Millonarios' goal was scored by Di Stéfano a few minutes after the indulgence of the referee.

The third final of the 1967 Intercontinental Cup between Celtic FC of Scotland and Racing Club of Argentina (they had each won their respective home matches in the "home and away" series) was a slaughter. The playoff, played on November 4 at the Centenario Stadium in Montevideo, had more boxing and wrestling than soccer. The 22 players proved to know a remarkable repertoire of punches and kicks that they distributed wholeheartedly, making officiating the match very difficult for the Paraguayan referee Rodolfo Pérez Osorio. As indicated (impartially) by the Spanish newspaper *El Mundo Deportivo,* "Äthe match has been very rough, with frequent violent actions and aggressions." The referee had extra work, since, in addition to having to deal with the language barrier that separated him from the Europeans, he had to red-card six players: Alfio Basile and Juan Carlos Rulli of the Argentine team, and Robert Lennox, John Hughes, James Johnstone, and Robert Auld of the Scottish side. However, the crucial match—won by Racing 1-0—ended with 17 men on the field. Why? Because Auld—a talented midfielder, hero of the European final played in Lisbon against FC Internazionale Milano of Italy—refused to leave the turf. Perez Osorio and the Celtic midfielder maintained a bitter "dialogue" that ended when the ref got tired and, because there were just mere seconds left and it seemed impossible to change the score, ordered the match to continue. With one more player, Racing controlled the play and won the first Intercontinental Cup for Argentine soccer. After the heated final, the officials of both squads showed very contradictory behavior: While Celtic fined each of their men 250 pounds for the embarrassing boxing display, the Racing players received a car per capita. For the triumph in the match, of course.

NAKED ACCUSATION

The coach of Itaperuna Esporte Clube de Brasil, Paulo Matta, exploded. In addition to suffering "a goal in offside" from the rival attacker Edmundo that gave the finishing touch to the 2-3 score at the Jair Bittencourt stadium in favor of Club de Regatas Vasco da Gama for the Copa Carioca of 1997, the referee José Carlos Santiago had red-carded three of his men. Furious at seeing his team and his work decimated, Matta jumped onto the field, approached the referee, and pulled down his pants to show him his ass. "I asked him if he also wanted it." The manager went berserk before the press microphones, which loved every minute of the unusual episode. "I got naked because I'm tired of working honestly just to be robbed so scandalously," said the nudist coach, adding that "soccer in Rio de Janeiro is a shame." After receiving a harsh 400-day suspension, Matta resolved to abandon his coaching career and start another...as a singer!

INTIMATE ENEMIES

CA Nueva Chicago was emerging as one of the favorites to win the Argentine Primera B (second tier) tournament in 1946. On the afternoon of April 27, they proved it at their Mataderos field by trouncing of CA Barracas Central, beating them comfortably 6 to 1. At 30 minutes into the second half, referee Carlos Mauri called a penalty for the home side. Oscar Meloni placed the ball in the white spot and started measuring the distance to kick, but before starting his run, the powerful defender Raúl Cocherari got in his way. "You already put two in, let me kick this one," demanded the defender. Meloni did not "shrink" and demanded that his partner move out of his way: "I am the man in charge." The dispute continued first with insults and then with blows, forcing the rest of the players of the "Little Bull" to separate the contenders and Mauri to expel them for reciprocal aggression. The completion of the kick, then, was not made by Meloni or Cocherari, but by Manuel Malachane, who from the twelve steps scored the seventh in Chicago that day. With two of their starters suspended because of their unusual incident, the green-and-black club lost the next game against CA Los Andes, broke their winning streak, and was left without the promotion at the end of the season, which was snatched by CA Banfield.

ON THE OTHER HAND

In March of 1998, the English city of Scarborough was the scene of one of the most exceptional penalties of all time. While Tap and Spile FC and Rangers Reserves FC faced each other in the local league in a very even match, referee Steve Ripley signaled a penalty shot for the visiting squad. Before one of the Rangers' players fired, Tap and Spile's captain, Paul Flack—enraged at the unfairness of the punishment—unleashed his anger in a very peculiar way: He got into his own penalty box and, after a short run, sent the ball to the net in the midst of a general stupor. Ripley should have invalidated the irregular goal because, according to the regulations, the kicker must be properly identified; the players of the defending team, except the goalkeeper, must remain outside the penalty box, behind the point of execution, and at least 10 yards from the ball; if any of these rules is violated, the shot must be repeated. However, the referee, angered by Flack's improper conduct, decided to approve the goal. Hard punishment for the transgressing captain: That afternoon, his team fell by 5 goals to 4!

RED TO GREEN

The referee Gary Bailey was bothered by the echo. Every time he whistled, there was an identical whistle emanating from the other side of the field, confusing everyone in the stadium of the English city of Hatfield, located about 25 miles north of London. Bailey blew his whistle, the game resumed, and the ghostly resonance stopped everything again. Thus, of course, the Herts Senior Centenary Trophy quarterfinal clash between Hertford Heath FC and Hatfield Town FC, could not continue.

Fed up with the struggle, the referee stopped the game to determine the source of the echo. He found it in a neighboring house: A Senegalese green parrot was having a great time imitating the man in black while watching the game from his cage! The feathered "Me-Too" was also the mascot of the local team. Possessing a sense of humor, Bailey went to the window and showed the bird his red card, which caused general laughter in the soccer players and the 150 spectators. Then, he rang the doorbell and asked the owner of the parrot, Irene Kerrigan, to move her pet to another part of the house until the end of the match, a request to which the woman agreed in a good humor. The annoying incident solved, the referee resumed play, and the game continued without new interference. Hatfield prevailed 5-2, and the eliminated Hertford Heath players argued bitterly that, undoubtedly, the defeat had been defined by the red card shown to Me-Too, their lucky charm.

WITHOUT A GOALIE

The Copa Roca was a contest played exclusively between Argentina and Brazil between 1914 and 1971, sporadically and altering its headquarters among Buenos Aires, Rio de Janeiro, and San Pablo. It was named as a tribute to former Argentine President Julio Roca, who at the beginning of the 1910s had performed an outstanding diplomatic maneuver to avoid wars between the two nations.

In January 1939, a sky blue-and-white team traveled to Rio de Janeiro twice to face their host foes at the São Januário Stadium. Although Brazil had just starred in a highly praised performance at the 1938 World Cup in Italy and had star striker Leônidas da Silva, who scored seven goals during that tournament, in the first match played on January 15, their rivals thrashed them without mercy, 1-5. The rematch one week later was more even: Leônidas opened the score, Bruno Rodolfi and Enrique García turned the score around, and, in the second half, Adilson Ferreira Antunes got the equalizer. At 86 minutes, a pass from Romeu Pellicciari to Adilson bounced in the hand of defender Sabino Coletta from the away team. The touch seemed unintentional, but the Brazilian referee Carlos de Oliveira Monteiro signaled the penalty spot, a fact that unleashed the anger of the Argentines. The goalkeeper Sebastián Gualco and the defender Arcadio López ran toward the referee and knocked him down, which brought in th police. What ultimately ensued was a reckless skirmish of batons, kicks, and fisticuffs that amazed the 70,000 spectators.

Outnumbered and outgunned, the away players retreated and took refuge in the locker room. However, the game did not end there: The referee, after an unprecedented decision, placed the ball on the 12-yard spot and ordered his compatriots to make the penalty effective, despite the fact that there was no goalkeeper in the Argentine goal! Without even blushing, striker José Perácio entered the box and fired a shot into the empty goal. With the score 3-2 and without an Argentine squad on the field, De Oliveira Monteiro whistled the end. While the Brazilians celebrated their "victory" on the pitch, their rivals took advantage to escape from the stadium with the Roca Cup in their possession, convinced that they had won it in lawfully after a win and a "draw."

KISSES

The Salto Uruguay FC club, the strongest team in the Uruguayan league, had the weak National FC pinned against their goal. All Salta players, except the goalkeeper, pushed toward the rival goal, whose players had desperately crowded the goal after the tie they needed to avoid relegation that same afternoon in June 1991. A few seconds from the end of the match, a long ball miraculously found Salto striker Sergio Leon, who, taking advantage of the carelessness of the defenders, was one-on-one with the unprotected goalkeeper in the most auspicious goal situation of the entire match. The attacker measured his shot, calculated where he wanted to place the ball, and kicked, but his shot went totally off target. Relief pervaded all the Nacional players, especially the defender Edgard Olivera, who should have been León's personal marker. Olivera approached his opponent and, in an extravagant demonstration of gratitude for what he considered a kindness, kissed his forehead. The rude gesture was noticed by the referee José Sequeira, who immpediately red-carded Olivera. Even with one man down, Nacional managed to escape the match with the tie. And even with the red card, Olivera celebrated, happy to have avoided relegation.

Center d'Esports L'Hospitalet needed a win against Unió Esportiva Figueres so as not to plunge to the bottom of the Spanish Second Division B. The Catalan club was close to achieving it on the afternoon of November 7, 1998, thanks to a goal from Peri Ventura, but the referee Carlos Clos Gomez granted a dubious penalty kick to the visiting team, which equalized the score and muted the Estadi de la Feixa Llarga. Ramón Moya, the hosts' manager, was desperate, and it was no wonder: He had only one victory in six games at home. However, after playing three minutes of additional time, with the draw seeming certain, a cross to the area found the head of defender Diego Martin, and he in turn found the net to pull L'Hospitalet ahead. The crowd—and Moya—erupted, and Moya torpedoed toward his bench to hug his assistants. Suddenly, the assistant referee Carmelo Bernat and the coach of the other team appeared in front of Moya, and. who knows why, stamped a huge kiss on his cheek. Bernat, perplexed, only managed to raise his flag to call Clos Gomez. After listening to the story of his collaborator, the referee took out his red card and ejected the affectionate man from the mach. After the game, when handing in the report, Clos Gómez described the kiss as "inappropriate." For Moya, however, it was different: "it's much better to do that than to throw stones at the referee or insult him." "The heart goes crazy sometimes, and I just can't control it," acknowledged the friendly and passionate coach.

Alessandro Veronese, scorer of the Italian team ASD Calcio Battaglia Terme, demonstrated why he had the reputation as a pickup artist in October 1996. In a match against La Rocca Monselice, played on the field of Via Reinaldi during the Veneto regional tournament, Veronese scored the second goal—and his second that afternoon—for his team with a powerful shot from 100 feet, which put the score at 2 to 1. To celebrate his double, the "artigliere" took off his blue-and-yellow shirt and hurled it. As he had already received one yellow card that day, the referee Anna de Toni showed Veronese another yellow and then the red card. The striker was astonished and, before leaving the field, approached the ref, shook her hand and gave her two kisses, one on each cheek. This action was written down by De Toni in her report, which was brought up to the Disciplinary Tribunal. After analyzing the case, the council disqualified the striker for two games, one more than what was usual for the consecutive yellows. In its resolution, the court determined that "the unusual act of trust toward the referee must be considered contrary to the regulation and punished with a day of suspension." A coherent failure: two goals, two cautions, two kisses, and two matches' penalty.

Veronese's punishment was light, if you compare that with the one received by his Dutch colleague Martin Bennink, although it should be noted that this gentleman kissed the referee on the mouth! Bennink, defender of the SV Wilhelminaschool's amateur squad of the city of Hengelo, was red-carded for vehemently protesting the referee's decisions and insulting him. "When they fuck with me, I like to kiss a lot," Bennink justified himself after planting one on the man in black's mouth. The Disciplinary Tribunal sentenced him to a suspension of eight matches for exercising "physical violence" and "assault on the dignity" of the referee.

The Spanish journalist Sergi Mas assures us that, in the 70s, the stadium Los Cármenes de Granada C.F. was the scene of a curious situation. Just after the game started between the home team and Real Madrid CF, the referee approached the coach of the host team and ejected him from the field. "Onto the street," said the man in black to the astonished coach, who had not insulted or committed any fault against anyone. The dizzying arbitrary decision was, in part, due, like the preceding stories, to passionate kisses. Although, in this case, between the coach and the wife of the referee. The ref took advantage of his investiture to take revenge on the person responsible for his having been made a cuckold. On returning to his house, the deceived used his red card again, but this time to throw his wife out of the bedroom.

CRAZY REACTIONS

Insults, blows, and spit are reactions as repulsive as they are "normal" after a red card. Nobody likes to leave the field before the match is done, and, with the heartbeats running up to a thousand beats per minute, violent behavior is today a common occurrence in all the world's stadiums. However, there are players who have proven to be more original than others when it comes to expressing their anger, such as the Argentine striker Sergio Ibarra. On February 25, 2000, after referee Carlos Hernandez— overseeing the Pesquero de Huancayo-FC Melgar of Arequipa match of the Peruvian First Division—exhibited his red card to the local player Lino Morán. Ibarra approached the man in black and...put his hand on his butt! The freehand man—or "free-fingered man"—was also red-carded and received a six-month punishment from the Justice Committee of the Sports Association (CJAD). Melgar won by a score of 3-0 although the match ended hastily after that: due to their inferiority both on the scoreboard and on the field, three men of Pesquero (today called Deportivo Wanka) simulated injuries for the match to end right there, so the win did not result in catastrophe.

More "playful," if the word fits, were the members of the amateur team Migliaro. In January of 2008, this squad of the Uruguayan department of Salto suffered five red cards to their rivals of the club Tío (meaning "Uncle," yes, that's their name!). As a repudiation of the red tide that had left them without the minimum regulatory amount of seven players to continue with the game, the players surrounded the referee Juan Carlos Silveira and, in a quick maneuver, took off his clothes. Stripped down to his underpants, the helpless referee was eventually rescued by the police.

Another one that did not have it easy was the referee Claudio Aranda in the second division match between Club de Deportes Antofagasta and Club de Deportes La Serena in April of 2003, by the second division. After the home team scored 2-1, La Serena's players furiously protested an alleged offside. In the middle of the tumultuous chaos, Aranda expelled the Argentine midfielder Rodrigo Riep. While the visitors continued with their claim, Riep saw that the referee had dropped the other card, the yellow one. Blind with anger, the former CA River Plate player took the card and, as if he had scissor hands, ripped it into a thousand pieces. "I broke it because I was really furious, I didn't even think about it, it was instinctual, I left it in pieces yes, and the card was made of plastic, but I was so mad and felt so wronged, that it felt like cardboard," Riep said. The consequence of this action, though, was that the Disciplinary Court gave the midfielder four suspension matches: one for the foul that motivated his expulsion from the game and three for his unusual reaction. "When I spoke with my old man and told him everything, he told me 'Kid, they sent you to jail there,'" he said with humor. His Italian colleague Fernando d'Ercoli had a similar, though slightly more "gourmet" attitude: after being thrown out in the ASD Pianta-ASD Ronta FC Arpax match, played in 1989 in a regional league, d'Ercoli snatched the red card from the ref…and ate it!

Meanwhile, Englishman Darren Painter's red card protest in November 1999 was a bit more disgusting. Defender for Buckland

Athletic FC of the Berkshire League, Painter approached the ref who had shown him the red card, took off his shorts, and urinated him! Of course, the foul reaction did not go unnoticed: Painter was thrown out of the league—and his own club—for life, and also from his own club.

RED CARD SUBSTITUTIONS

On February 8, 2000, in Prenton Park, the host team, Tranmere Rovers FC (part of the Premier Division) defeated Sunderland AFC of the Premier League, 1-0, in the fourth round of the FA English Cup thanks to a goal by Wayne Allison in the 25th minute. A few minutes from the end, with Sunderland rallying against the Rovers in pursuit of the equalizer, defender Clint Hill committed a bad foul inches from the Tranmere penalty box. The referee Rob Harris called the foul and expelled Hill because of his violent play. Coincidentally, a few seconds earlier, coach John Aldridge had ordered Stephen Frail to substitute in for Hill. When the defender approached the middle line, fourth official David Unsworth, who had not noticed the ejection, allowed Frail to enter for his teammate. All the confusion overwhelmed Harris, who didn't see the sub join the defenders. Tranmere continued with their eleven players for a few seconds until visiting coach Peter Reid alerted the referee. Seeing his mistake and that of his assistant, Harris sent Frail back to his place among the substitutes. Tranmere finally won, 1-0.

Two days later, the competition supervisory committee confirmed the result and absolved the winning team of any fault. Meanwhile, the committee suspended the referee for a match despite his having been assigned to officiate the cup clash between Gillingham FC and Bradford City AFC. The committee justified the mistake by saying that "the referee and his assistants were under a considerable level of pressure," and told Sunderland that "their decisions are final, and for the good of the game, they must be accepted." The red-and-white club not only accepted them, but, in an unusual gesture, Peter Reid told the press that "according to our point of view it is not the best decision, but we abide by it. I wish John [Aldridge] and his people good luck, and all the best against Fulham." Tranmere continued their run and in the next round beat Fulham FC, also in the first division, 2 to 1. Unfortunately in the next match, they fell 3 to 2 against the powerful Newcastle United FC.

An almost identical situation had happened before, only it ended a bit differently. On January 10, 1937, during the Copa America held in Argentina, the host team defeated Peru 1-0 in the San Lorenzo de Almagro CA. During the game, despite the field goal by the Estudiantes CA de La Plata striker Alberto Zozaya, the team wasn't doing very well. The visiting team attacked on all fronts in pursuit of the equalizer. At the 84th minute, the Uruguayan referee Aníbal Tejada ejected defender Antonio Sastre from the match. According to the media, this ejection was unjustified, but, despite the ruling, Argentina continued playing the game with eleven men.

Remember that until 1968, the yellow and red cards did not exist, and the referees reported their decisions "by word," with a hand gesture that wasn't always easy to notice from a distance. As Sastre approached the sideline, the Argentine coach Manuel Seoane, in a quick and skillful maneuver, made Hector Blotto enter as a "sub" for the expelled teammate. Tejada did not see the stratagem, and his assistant referees and the Peruvian bench naively assumed that it was a conventional replacement (at that time, substitutions in league championships were not allowed, but the regulation of the South American Football Confederation did authorize them for this tournament) and didn't report the incident to the referee. All things being equal, the Argentina squad resisted the Peruvian attack and ended the encounter victorious. This result was key for the hosts, which ended the round robin play with Brazil in first place with eight points. If Peru had equalized, the trophy would have traveled directly to Rio de Janeiro in the hands of the men managed by Adhemar Pimenta. But, when the draw was registered, a playoff final was scheduled for February 1, again at the San Lorenzo stadium. And, there, Argentina beat Brazil 2-0 and lifted the Copa América for the fifth time.

IN WOMEN'S CLOTHING

Bolivian Club Deportivo Jorge Wilstermann fans were infuriated at Paraguayan club Olimpia's 1-0 lead. The two teams were playing in a crowded Félix Capriles stadium in the city of Cochabamba that night, March 29, 1979, for the Copa Libertadores. Hugo Talavera's goal at 15 minutes practically eliminated the "aviator" team, although only two matches had been disputed. At that time, only one team per zone advanced to the semifinals. In need of a draw and technically overcome by their rival, the Bolivians began to use force. The game became very violent, and soon the match resembled more a massive boxing melee than a soccer game.

At eleven minutes into the second half, with the score still 0-1, the Bolivians became embroiled in a pitched battle that could only be contained with police force. When peace returned, Brazilian referee José Roberto Wright took the red card out of his pocket to expel a single Olimpia player, forward Enrique Atanasio Villalba, and four Wilstermann men: the defenders Carlos Arias, Miguel Bengolea, and Raúl Navarro and the attacker Juan Sánchez. According to the report, one of the expelled players from Wilstermann had launched "a flying kick, looking for the body of the rival." The unequal justice rendered by Wright for an "everyone against everyone" fight angered the spectators even more, but the real disaster occurred a few minutes later when, favored by the numerical inferiority of their opponent, Evaristo Isasi scored Olimpia's second goal.

To avoid a blow out, the coach for the Bolivian team, Roberto Pavisic, ordered one of his men to "get injured," leaving the team with only six players. Since there were no more substitutions for the decimated Wilstermann, Wright was forced to whistle the end of the match twenty minutes prior to time because the Bolivian club did not have a minimum of seven players required by regulation. The story, however, did not end there.

Hundreds of disgruntled fans invaded the field and ran after the Olimpia players and, mainly, the referee, to gratify their need for revenge for what they considered a tremendous injustice. The police could do little to contain the anger of so many people. Several of Olimpia's players received unmitigated punching and kicking. Assisted by a handful of policemen, the Paraguayans managed to escape the mob and lock themselves in their dressing room. Wright and his assistants, meanwhile, had to remain in their dressing room for several hours because the stadium had been surrounded by hundreds of outraged spectators. As revealed by Wilstermann midfielder Johnny Villarroel many years later during an interview, the only way Wright would leave the stadium was disguised as a woman. The Brazilian and his collaborators were taken to the city of Oruro more than 125 miles from Cochabamba, because they were told that a crowd of fans was waiting for the referee at the Cochabamba airport.

Because of this incident, CONMEBOL suspended the Felix Capriles stadium for a long time and ejected the five players. Club Jorge Wilstermann played the two remaining games at home in Santa Cruz de la Sierra and La Paz. They lost them, too.

Olimpia, meanwhile, went to the next round: they won the group, then the semifinal, and, in the final, lifted the Copa Libertadores after dethroning the Argentine champion, Boca Juniors. Wright, meanwhile, would experience another very dark night in this continental tournament two years later, but that story is still to come.

INOPPORTUNE

What kind of record can a goalkeeper of the Botswana national team have? A very unique one, as it turns out. Goalkeeper Modiri Marumo, who was also the captain of "the zebras," was the only player ever to receive a red card during a penalty shootout. Crazy, yes, but real. During the Castle Cup played in South Africa in 2003, the Botswana versus Malawi match ended in a 1-1 draw. Referee Mateus Infante from Mozambique called for the game to be decided from the twelve yards. The singular incident occurred after Malawian Philip Nyasulu scored the third goal of the series for his team. Nyasulu approached the defeated Marumo and gave him a pat on the shoulder, which Marumo answered with a blow to Nyasulu's face. Infante, of course, showed the red card to the goalkeeper for his improper reaction. "I reacted badly; I am committed to make sure this does not happen again. I behaved inappropriately which embarrasses me. I hope my apologies will be accepted, and I will be able to serve my nation again," Marumo said to the press. How did the series of penalties continue? Botswana missed the next shot, and Malawian Ganizani Malunga sealed the victory for his country by beating Michael Mogaladi, a defender who had to guard the goal in place of the expelled goalkeeper.

LIVE

Soccer and radio maintain a powerful and almost centennial romance. So deeply rooted are the games' transmissions that many fans turn down the volume on their television and turn up the volume their radios to follow the images on the screen with the narration of their favorite play-by-play radio announcer. Others go to the stadium with their headphones on to hear someone describe what they are watching. But nothing is as unusual as a soccer player following the circumstances of a game on the radio...while he's playing!

On October 11, 1992, at La Bombonera, CA Boca Juniors (who hadn't won an Argentine championship for eleven years) received their bitter "superclásico" rival, CA River Plate. The *xeneize* squad was at the top of the standings with 14 points, followed closely by its biggest enemy with 13. At 65 minutes, Boca was up 1-0 thanks to a goal from Uruguayan Sergio Martinez. Then, referee Juan Carlos Lousteau called a foul; one of the well-known "divers," *millionaire* Ariel Ortega, master of the art of falling down, was sandwiched between defenders, Carlos MacAllister and Alejandro Giuntini from the host team. A Boca supporter, enraged by the referee's decision, threw his small yellow radio at the rival goalkeeper, Ángel Comizzo. The device fell within three feet of the goalie, who had the smart idea of taking it, putting on the headphones, and following the call of the radio announcers to hear Hernán Díaz's shot from twelve yards, with his back to the play and in front of the opposing fans. But the powerful crossed shot of Diaz was rejected by the hands of the Boca number "1," Carlos Navarro Montoya, and Comizzo, enraged, plucked the small speakers from his ears and threw the fateful apparatus toward the wire fence. The match finished without further displays of emotion, and Boca maintained the 1-0 advantage. At the end of that Sunday, the club from the port extended its advantage over River by three points, which allowed them to win the championship a few weeks later and leave their historic adversary empty handed.

UNEXPECTED SCORERS

Throughout the years, there have been several goalkeepers who scored goals in unusual circumstances. Just arrived at the London club Arsenal FC from Old Ham Athletic AFC, Frank Moss snatched the starting position from legendary goalkeeper Charlie Preedy to win three straight titles with the Gunners: 1932-33, 1933-34, and 1934-35. In that last season, Arsenal won a difficult match in their visit to Goodison Park, Everton FC's field, on March 16, 1935. In the first half, with the score blank, Moss fell badly during a play and dislocated his left shoulder. As substitutions were not allowed then, the goal was occupied by a field player. The goalkeeper was taken to the locker room, where his shoulder was bandaged, and, after halftime, he returned to the pitch to play as a forward. In his new position, Moss scored Arsenal's first goal that afternoon, and ultimately Arsenal would leave the pitch victorious, with a final score of 2-0. The feat, nevertheless, did not compensate the goalie's misfortune: The dislocation was so severe that Moss could only play in five more matches before retiring at the age of 27.

A similar (practically identical) event happened on August 31, 1962, when the English club Reading FC received Halifax Town AFC in Elm Park for a Third Division match. The host goalkeeper, Arthur Wilkie, hurt his hand, left his place to a partner, and went on to play in the attack: He scored two goals for Reading who won 4-2!

THE DISGUISE

Uruguayan forward Julio César Britos Vázquez (known from his career with CA Peñarol and Real Madrid CF and as world champion in Brazil 1950, although he did not play a game) played a bit mischievously, allowing him to score lots of goals. However, one time, a dose of trickery mixed dangerously with a pinch of inexperience, teaching him a tough but valuable lesson.

In 1943, while participating in a derby against Nacional in the youth division of the Uruguayan league, Britos Vázquez, who played with a white beret (many players from Rio de la Plata wore berets so the stitching on the old balls wouldn't hurt their heads), was expelled during the first half of the heated match. At halftime, the attacker asked his coach if he could return to the field to play in the match Peñarol was losing. The coach, aware that Britos Vázquez was his best offensive weapon, agreed, although he asked him how he would disguise his unlawful return. The boy, audacious as ever, took off his beret, unfolded his long hair, tucked his shirt inside his pants and raised his socks. The new appearance of the forward seemed convincing to the coach and the rest of the young players, and the clever striker returned to the field. The referee and the rival team looked with surprise at the "substitute," who they couldn't identify even though his face seemed familiar. Who did notice the trick, however, was an observer who, coincidentally, knew Britos Vázquez from the neighborhood. The young man was therefore suspended for six months after being found guilty of...impersonating himself!

AL DENTE

The referee Henning Erikstrup checked his watch. The match had come to an end, and on that afternoon, April 18, 1960, it seemed Nørager IF had beaten Ebeltoft IF 4-3 in the tournament of Denmark's Fourth Division. As he began to blow the whistle to signal the end of the match, Eirkstrup had a bit of a surprise. The referee's dentures took advantage of the slight parting of his lips to suddenly escape. Erikstrup dropped quickly to pick up his fallen teeth and save himself from the embarrassing situation. Right at that moment—while the referee was otherwise engaged—the away team scored the equalizer. The men from Ebeltoft started a lively celebration, but the referee cut it short by refusing to allow the goal, because he, in fact, hadn't seen it. The furious Ebeltoft players surrounded Erikstrup, demanding to know why he refused to count the goal. The poor referee had no choice but to admit that he prioritized his self-esteem before his officiating duties. One of the players asked him why he didn't whistle the end of the match and then pick up his teeth. "I had to recover the prosthetic enhancement before anyone stepped on it and destroyed it; it's very expensive," Erikstrup apologized, his face redder than his card.

YELLOW, RED, AND BLACK

The rules of the game are as simple as they are clear, and the referee has the absolute authority to enforce them. But what happens when the referee appears to completely ignore the regulations? In March 2002, in the Brazilian state of Piauí, referee Edmílson Timoteo da Silva showed three yellow and two red cards to the same player. The unusual case, which occurred during a match between local teams Ríver Atlético Clube and Oeiras Atlético Clube, began with a sharp tackle from the away team's defender, Paulo Araujo, who justly deserved a yellow card. A minute later, Araujo performed another hard tackle and was reprimanded. As was fairly common knowledge, yellow plus yellow equals red, and so it was on this day. Although, in this case, the defender, instead of going to the showers, stayed on the field, and the game went on without the referee, his assistants, or the snoozing players of Ríver and their managerial staff noticing the irregular maneuver. As the rude Araujo had apparently not yet quenched his thirst for blood, he soon after tackled another a rival player. Da Silva, this time more cautious, showed him the third yellow and the second—and final—red. At the end of the match, the referee argued that he had confused Araujo with one of his teammates because of his physical resemblance. A silly argument, if one considers that the other player had not left the field with the first red.

A slightly more serious instance of a ref, Englishman Graham Poll, disregarding regulation took place during the 2006 World

Cup in Germany surrounded by the highest television technology and before millions of viewers. During the clash between Croatia and Australia, played on June 22 in Stuttgart, Poll showed three yellow cards to European defender Josip Simunic. The defender saw the first warning in the 61st minute and the second in the 90th, but continued playing on the field without the referee or his assistants noticing. Finally, in the 93rd minute, Simunic protested a call by the referee and won himself the third yellow, which was followed by a red card. The regulation gives the referee the possibility of modifying his decision if he realizes that it is incorrect. In these two cases, the men in black acted with an amazing ineffectiveness. Unfortunately, they were not the only ones.

IT'S TIME, REF!

When the referee Luis Ventre blew the final whistle, the eleven players of CA Estudiantes de La Plata embraced to celebrate an unlikely win against Racing Club, the leader of the 1957 Argentine championship and in their very own Avellaneda home. However, like all good things, the sweet celebration didn't last. While players and fans were leaving the field, one of the linemen warned Ventre that the clock had been advanced and that there were still five minutes left to play. Upon noticing his mistake, the referee summoned the players and ordered play to resume by dropping ball, as regulation indicates. The visitors reluctantly accepted the measure. A few seconds later, their discontent turned into anger, because in those few moments, "the Academy" achieved a definitive equalizer from a thunderous strike by Juan José Kellemen.

What happened to the watch of the English referee Thomas Saywell? On November 26, 1898, the referee ended the match between Millwall FC and Southampton FC of the old English Southern League ten minutes early! The managers of the host team Millwall FC protested and demanded that the league authorities reconvene the two squads to dispute the remaining time. They were bent on the idea that their squad could equalize the adverse score in that span of time. The court heard the claim and rescheduled the short match...for almost five months later! The Southampton men bitterly accepted the decision, and on

April 12, 1899, they traveled the 65 miles (100 kilometers) to the Dell Stadium in the center of London on the edge of the Thames to complete the match. After so many qualms, the ten minutes were played without a change in the score, which became official: Millwall 1, Southampton 4...

THREE MATCHES IN A DAY

Grêmio Foot-Ball Porto Alegrense, a team from the Brazilian city of Porto Alegre and world club champion in 1983, made world soccer history by playing an unprecedented three games in a single day. The strange event, which took place on Sunday, December 11, 1994, was the product of Grêmio's busy schedule; that year they had participated in the Brazilian championship—which schedules matches twice a week—the regional tournament of the state of Rio Grande do Sul, the South American Super Cup, and the Copa Conmebol. The three commitments, qualifiers for the Rio Grande do Sul regional tournament of 1995, took place one after the other with an interval of only fifteen minutes. Despite the exhausting marathon, the Grêmio team won two (4 to 3 against Santa Cruz and 1 to 0 against Brazil de Pelotas) and had one draw (no goals against Aimore). For the occasion, the coach Luiz Felipe employed 33 players, of which three took part in two of the matches. On the other hand, barely 247 fans witnessed the three matches, even though the entry ticket—at regular price—allowed the participants to remain in the stadium throughout the day.

A MOMENT OF SILENCE

The intense cold and his 85 years did not stop Fred Cope from watching his beloved "bears" of Congleton Town Football Club, a team that competes in the North West Counties' Regional League of England. On February 27, 1993, the same as every time his beloved team of black and white jerseys performed at home, Cope went to the Booth Street stadium and sat in one of the seats of their small stands. At the appointed time, Congleton and his opponent, which was Rossendale United that day, took to the field and prepared for the kickoff. The referee blew his whistle, and the 22 protagonists froze with their heads lowered in a respectful "moment of silence." The attendees, respectfully, stood up to acknowledge the tribute. While getting up, Fred asked his seat neighbor who was being honored? The man looked at him, and, beginning to smile, replied: "You!" The old man thought it was a joke, but the magazine with the match program was very clear, reporting the death of the oldest of the Congleton Town fans: Fred Cope. "I've been sick this week, but it wasn't that bad," Fred replied. The strange situation soon became known throughout the audience, who forced the editor of the publication, Chris Phillips, to appear before Cope to apologize. "Excuse me, but the secretary had informed me that you were dead, so I posted it on the program and asked the referee for a minute of silence," Phillips blushed. Despite the blunder, the day ended happily: Congleton Town thrashed the away team 6-1, and the veteran fan won 10 pounds in the traditional draw of halftime. Don't worry, dear reader, the raffle wasn't fixed...

HALF-THRASHED

On May 4, 1935, Exeter City FC thrashed Aldershot Town FC 8 to 1 at their home of St. James Park on the last day of the tournament of the Third English Southern Division. So far, the information does not seem too relevant. The detail that makes this story curious is that the first half of this match was 0-0!

A CLOSE 9-0

One of the greatest successes of the English club Newcastle United FC was to win the 1931/32 FA Cup. In the final match, the team from the north of England defeated Arsenal FC 2-1 at the majestic Wembley Stadium in London on April 23, 1932, in the presence of more than 92,000 people. During Newcastle's long but triumphant journey, they experienced one very remarkable episode: In the fourth round, this first division team faced Southport FC, a modest squad from the third tier that had just eliminated Barnsley FC with a decided 4-1. The duel was set for January 23, 1932, at St. James Park, the opulent home of Newcastle United, where, despite the abysmal divisional difference, the match ended 1-1. Three days later, the tiebreaker was played at the Merseyrail Community Stadium, the quaint Southport home. There, the score was again 1-1. On the first of February, Newcastle United and Southport met again at St. James Park to decide the tie. And, as the third time's the charm, the clash was won by the Newcastle FC, who finally got rid of their tenacious opponent with a result that seemed undeniably unusual after two even draws: 9-0.

FUNNY

After two notorious absences—Brazil 1949 and Peru 1953—the Argentine national team returned to the Copa America, which took place at the National Stadium in Santiago, Chile, in 1955. The sky blue-and-white team was led by Guillermo Stábile. As manager, Stábile received two records that, at the close of this tournament, remained uncontested: more titles won—seven: Chile 1941, Chile 1945, Argentina 1946, Ecuador 1947, Chile 1955 , Peru 1957, and the Pan-American Cup Costa Rica 1960—and more managed games: 44, all with the same team. In Santiago, Argentina started with two wins (5-3 against Paraguay and 4-0 against Ecuador) and a draw at two goals per side with Peru. The fourth match, on March 27, was another huge display against a bitter rival, Uruguay. At 76 minutes, the Stábile team was already winning 5 to 1. At minute 80, the coach decided to make a change: the offensive midfielder Norberto Conde for center forward Angel Labruna, who had scored two goals. As soon as he stepped on the grass, Conde, who was making his debut with the sky blue and white, approached the tough Uruguayan defender Matías González and sarcastically asked him: "Dude, how's the match going?" Gonzalez, who was already boiling because of the adverse result, responded with a terrible punch that knocked Conde out. The Uruguayan was expelled; the joker, passed out in the dressing room. Labruna reentered—as regulation allowed—and scored his third goal at minute 87, which rounded off a score of 6 to 1, the biggest win of the Rio de la Plata derby. On the last day, Argentina defeated the local squad 1 to 0 and celebrated with the Olympic lap. Conde? He didn't get on the pitch…just in case.

To play the FA English Cup of 1887/88, Aston Villa FC put together a very competitive team. For the first round of the championship on October 15, 1887, the Birmingham club beat Oldbury Town FC 4-0. Then, on November 5, they beat Small Heath Alliance FC by the same score. The team went through to the third stage without competing, and on December 17, for the fourth round, the Scottish team Shankhouse FC was overwhelmed by 9 to 0. The reports of the time have it that Villa's dominance was so overwhelming that, in the middle of the match, a spectator handed a chair to the bored goalkeeper James Warner. It is claimed that Warner followed the rest of the match without having to leave his seat. The streak of the Birmingham squad was stopped in the round of 16 when they fell to Preston North End FC by 3 to 1. This time, Warner had a lot of work, since he had to go to find the ball at the back of the net three times.

A few years later, in 1901, AC Milan traveled to the province of Pavia to face the Lombard team Casteggio FC for the Italian Negrotto Cup. The Englishman Herbert Kilpin, player, captain, and one of the founders of the Milanese team, said in his memoirs: "Davis was our goalkeeper. Foreseeing that it was an easy game, Davis did not change and went out with a chair, and he was sitting comfortably, one leg over the other, with his straw hat on his head and smoking cigarettes without stopping, and in the end, bored, he asked me: 'Can I play a little too?' Laughing, I let him out of the goal. Davis mixed in with the forwards and scored our twentieth goal." Milan won 20-0, and, according to Kilpin, his teammate scored the first goal by a goalkeeper in Italian soccer.

A FIELD OF SAND

According to the prestigious magazine *Forbes,* Manchester United FC is the richest soccer club in the world and is only surpassed by the New York Yankees baseball team. However, the origin of this powerful English institution is in a modest team called Newton Heath, located in the neighborhood of northeastern Manchester. On Saturday, March 9, 1895, Newton Heath FC hosted Walsall Town Swifts FC for the English second division tournament at its humble Bank Street stadium, which looked nothing like the now fantastic Old Trafford, the "theater of dreams." In fact, that afternoon, the groundskeeper of the rudimentary stadium had to use several shovelfuls of sand to cover the puddles left by an untimely storm. At the moment of the initial whistle, the terrain had just a few bushes of grass in the middle of a muddy mixture of mud and gravel. The visiting players agreed to enter that inhospitable field, although they had the foresight to say that they did it "under protest." Its men sunk in the mud, Walsall Town Swifts suffered an undisputable defeat of 14 to 0. Well, not really so undisputable. After the singular encounter, the thrashed squad protested against the poor state of the field to the Football League. The organization accepted the claim, annulled the result, and ordered that the game be replayed from minute zero on the same field on the following Wednesday. This second time, with the field in better conditions, the actions were much more even. Newton Heath won by only...9 to 0!

DROWNED GOALS

"Soccer is not mathematics. Two plus two rarely gives four. You can get three, five, and even zero," Dutch coach Leo Beenhakker once said. It doesn't seem a crazy thought, especially if you consider that an effective striker scored seven goals for his team to lose...3-1! No, this is not a typo. This happened even though none of those seven goals was canceled by the referee. How was it possible? Through the intricate paths on which the ball rolls. On January 28, 1961, during the fourth round of the prestigious FA English Cup, Manchester City FC won 6-2 with all six goals scored by their star attacker, Scotsman Denis Law. At 21 minutes from the end, a torrential rain flooded the Kenilworth Road stadium, and referee Ken Tuck had to suspend the match. According to the tournament regulation, if the game was interrupted by a circumstance outside of the normal play, the match had to be played again and with a blank score. Four days later, with the field in better conditions, Law scored once again for City, but that day Luton recovered and, with a better outcome, won 3-1. The water had diluted the victory of Manchester. Because that first match was suspended, it was not officially recorded, and Law could not count any of his goals. Had he been able to, his name would have remained on the history books as the top scorer of the tournament in the twentieth century.

SHAME AWAY

In the mid-1950s, Real Madrid CF put together one of the greatest teams in history, winning five European Champions Clubs' Cup—origin of the current UEFA Champions League— in a row thanks to the magic of exceptional soccer players like Argentinean Alfredo di Stéfano, French Raymond Kopa, and Hungarian Ferenc Puskás. To present the small French forward—the son of Polish immigrants, whose real name was Kopaszewski—the Madrid club organized a friendly match with a team from the French first division, Football Club Sochaux-Montbéliard, on October 4, 1956, at the Santiago Bernabéu stadium. That afternoon, di Stéfano and Kopa played as if they had played together for years. The Argentinean (who scored four goals) and the Frenchman (who scored three) led a wonderful tournament that culminated in a triumphant 14-1. The wide "Viking" victory did not cause much pleasure beyond the Pyrenees. Although it had been a friendly game, the French Federation took the humiliation very seriously and forbade Sochaux to leave the country for a whole year.

JUST BECAUSE YOU THRASH A TEAM DOESN'T MEAN...

Serbian coach Vujadin Boškov once said: "I'd rather lose one match 9-0 than nine 1-0." Of course, Boškov may have had a reason for saying this. His team, Real Madrid CF, had just fallen 9-1 to FC Bayern München in a friendly played in 1980. Beyond its context, this maxim denotes remarkably practical logic. It can also be said that it's better to win ten matches by 1-0 than one match by 10 goals. On June 15, 1982, during the World Championship played in Spain, Hungary crushed El Salvador 10-1, which up until today was the biggest win in the history of the competition. That day, Magyar Laszlo Kiss became the most effective substitute in a Cup match, scoring three goals during the 35 minutes he was on the field before being replaced by Andras Torocsik. Unfortunately for the European squad, such a fantastic victory did not help: After falling to Argentina (4-1) and taking a draw with Belgium (1-1), Hungary fell to third place in Group 3 and bid farewell to the tournament in the first round.

Speaking of World Cups and Hungary, another example of excessive useless thrashing came from the Magyar squad during the 1954 Cup in Switzerland when they were the top scorers with 27 goals in just six games. Ten of those goals were scored against Germany. In the first round, Hungary beat the German squad 8 to 3. It was the fate of these two teams to qualify for the second round and meet again in the final. There, the Magyar team achieved a quick advantage of 2 to 0. But, as the match went on, that advantage evaporated and ended with a 3-2 win for Germany, who achieved its first World Cup final win.

Another alarming case occurred during the Korea–Japan 2002 qualifier. Australia got the record win for an official international match by beating American Samoa 31-0 on April 11, 2001 at the International Sports Stadium in Coffs Harbor, New South Wales. However, the overwhelming Australian power was punctured a few months later when the yellow jersey team, winner of the Oceania group, faced Uruguay in the playoff against South America. Australia won 1-0 at home, but in Montevideo, their supposed strength was dampened in front of the famous *Charrúa* grittiness. The "Socceroos" lost 3-0 and left without a cup.

In France on June 24, 1998, Spain thrashed Bulgaria 6-1 on the last match day for group D. The huge difference in the score line did not help; the red team was eliminated because it could barely reach the third place in the group, behind Nigeria and Paraguay, both of whom qualified for the next round. Twelve years later, in South Africa 2010, Spain was a brilliant champion with barely 8 goals in 7 games. From the round of 16, they successively beat Portugal, Paraguay, Germany, and Holland with the same score: 1-0. Undoubtedly, the Iberian team had learned a lot about the "Boškov rule."

PARTY

A thrashing is obvious when there is a wide difference in score between both contenders. This disparity may occur at the technical and tactical level, in the physical condition of the players, in one or more ejections that unbalance the teams, or even in a bribe. Other times, when the score exceeds seven or eight goals, it's clear the game suffered some extraordinary circumstance that eluded all expectations of directors, coaches, and even the players themselves. If you don't believe me, just ask Namibia. The girls of the African women's national team, known as the "valiant gladiators," were in awe over their rooms at their hotel in the South African city of Johannesburg. It was the first time that they participated in an Olympic qualifier (to participate in Athens 2004) and to be lodged in such a magnificent place was already a triumph. So much so, that the girls forgot why they were there and threw themselves, uninhibited, into enjoying the room service. The party started with drinks and sweets and, when the temperature rose, it led to the rental of six porn films. The next day, October 24, 2003, the Namibian girls had a very bad time on the field. Exhausted, they could not prevent their South African rivals from scoring without mercy and winning 13-0. When they heard about the bacchanalia—word of the hotel festivities had gotten out, exposing the party girls—the Namibia higher-ups decided to punish the players and, for the away match in Windhoek, the capital of Namibia, on November 7, they decided to make the pre-game stay in an austere cloister stripped of televisions and hotel room bars. More concentrated and better rested, the "valiant gladiators" got a much better result, although they fell anyway, 0-8.

A LORD OF THE RING

A few years ago, FIFA added a provision to the regulations related to players' clothing: "Players will not use any equipment or carry any object that is dangerous to themselves or to other players (including any kind of jewel)." In 2000, this provision was not yet regulation, which is a pity, because it could have prevented a sharp headache for Brazilian Vítor Rivaldo Borba Ferreira. On May 27 of that year, the talented midfielder played with his team in a friendly match against England at the traditional Wembley stadium. During the middle of the game, Rivaldo noticed a disappointing loss: the wedding ring he used to kiss after each goal—a thick piece of gold with his wife's name, Eliza, engraved on it—had escaped from his left hand ring finger to disappear on 7,350 square meters of pitch at the legendary stadium. The Brazilian, disconcerted, spent the rest of the match more concerned about recovering his ring than kicking the ball. After the match, which ended 1-1, Rivaldo showered and, upon reaching the bus that would take the South American squad to the airport, was pleasantly surprised by a Wembley employee, who returned his precious jewel. The ring had been found on the lawn by one of the English soccer players, defender Martin Keown. Rivaldo returned home very relieved, but, fearing a new setback with a different outcome, he tattooed the name of his beloved Eliza on the ring finger of his left hand.

A SEAGULL'S ASSIST!

The kids of the English Hollingworth Juniors FC youth team had all the markings of an unbeatable team, so the attack led by Danny Worthington of the rival squad, Stalybridge Celtic FC, seemed inconsequential. Without a free pass, Worthington decided to shoot toward the goal, but his powerful shot went very high and was fated to go well past the goal. But, at that moment, a seagull was flying over the field. The ball hit the seagull full on and went straight into the net of the Hollingworth Juniors. Amazing! This youth league match was played in September 1999 in the English city of Manchester, and the referee, wrongly, endorsed the extraordinary goal. Demoralized after playing 11 against 12, the boys of Hollingworth fell 7-1. "I could not believe it; everyone came to congratulate me for the goal, but the bird was the one who really scored it," said 13-year-old Danny Worthington. His status had changed from "gunner" to "assist." The gull, meanwhile, did not celebrate its goal. After falling stunned on the pitch, it recovered and flew away. No one was able to ask the bird its name to engrave it in the marble of history.

WHAT A PAIR!

During the inaugural edition of the Coupe de Championnat, the first division league of Belgium, 1895/96, Racing Football Club of Brussels, second in the standings and a big candidate for the title, received the weak Union Football Club of Ixelles, which, until that day, November 24, 1895, had not won or tied any game. Racing (which after bankruptcies and other vicissitudes was transformed into the current Koninklijke Football Club Rhodienne-Verrewinkel) went out to eat their rival raw and rallied constantly all the first half, unable to open the score or suffer a single counterattack of their fragile opponent. In the second half, the local squad maintained its control of the ball, to the point that their goalkeeper, Gustave Pelgrims, very bored, took a reserve ball that was next to his goal and began to play with a partner. The distraction was taken advantage of by one of the boys of Union, who tried a strong shot from his own field. Helped a bit by its power and direction, and a little by a strong burst, the ball flew over the home team's field and landed inside Pelgrims' goal, who was still playing with the extra ball. After spitting a torrent of insults at their unproductive goalkeeper, the surprised Racing players tried to equalize the score, but they were unsuccessful. After the final whistle, the young visitors celebrated their only triumph of the tournament: after 12 matches, Union had 1 victory and 11 defeats, with 5 goals in favor and 51 against, and finished in seventh place among seven teams. This club from Ixelles, a neighborhood in the south of Brussels, did not participate in the next championship—it preferred to continue in less demanding competitions—until in 1901, it disappeared. Much like Pelgrims' reputation.

NOSY FLAG

To prevent the television cameras from revealing that the stadium of the Peruvian team Deportivo Municipal de Chorrillos had no grandstand behind one of the goals, the president of the club, Ricardo Belmont, decided that in each home game six fans would go up to the wall that closed that sector of the stadium and, during the match, would cover it with a huge flag with the club's white and red colors. The initiative pleased everyone, not only because the measure hid that ugly part but also because, in a way, it gave color and warmth to a property that was going to be the headquarters of the 1994 First Division Decentralized Tournament.

The games were happening without a glitch and, in each of them, the local fans celebrated every time their beloved banner was unfurled. That is, they did until Saturday, May 28. That day, when Municipal received Social Club and Deportivo Carlos A. Mannucci for the ninth match of the tournament, the flag wanted to be a protagonist on the other side of the end line. Twenty-eight minutes into the second half, with the scoreboard still blank, host striker Ricardo Besada moved swiftly to the right, sending a precise cross to his teammate, Alfredo Carmona. At that moment, a strong breeze blew, ripping the huge fabric from the hands of the fans and blew it toward the field, wrapping it around Mannucci's goal. Carmona took a shot. The ball passed the away goalkeeper Oscar Ibáñez and traveled straight to the net but was stopped by the fluttering flag. The Municipal flag prevented Municipal's goal. The regulation warns that, in the face of unforeseen situations of these characteristics, when there's participation of agents outside the game, the referee must order a dropped ball. However, the referee Alberto Tejada, perhaps more pragmatically, awarded the goal to the squad that played at home. The Mannucci players spouted lukewarm protests until they accepted the ruling. Municipal won 1-0 with that controversial goal. Belmont decided not to renew the contract to the white and red banner. Maybe he should have placed another flag in black, in tribute to the ref.

BEACH SOCCER

It was understandably called "the most unlikely goal in the history of English soccer." On October 17, 2009, Sunderland AFC received Liverpool FC at their Stadium of Light for the ninth round of the English Premier League 2009/10. Five minutes after initiating action, with Sunderland on the attack, Irishman Andy Reid sent a cross from the right; Frenchman Steed Malbranque deflected it with his heel; and English Darren Bent pulled a big right strike that did not seem too difficult for the experienced hands of the kneeling José "Pepe" Reina, the Spanish goalkeeper for the away squad. However, the shot became deadly when the ball deflected...off a beach ball, a red one, which was rolling haphazardly through the Liverpool penalty box. Reina, surprised, was frozen, unable to react to the singular circumstance. The soccer ball passed him on his left and stuck in the net; the beach ball eluded him on his right and came out at the end line. The referee, Mike Jones, should have annulled the goal, but he did not, so he was punished by the FA for one match. Because of the speed of the action, which disconcerted Jones and didn't allow him to stop the attack before it ended in a goal, the referee should have overruled the goal because the beach ball got in the way of its soccer "cousin."

The eccentric event was aggravated by two, not inconsequential, circumstances: the first, that Sunderland won the match 1-0; the second, that the red ball had been thrown to the field by a...

Liverpool fan! Callum Campbell, 16, admitted to the newspaper *The Sunday Mirror* that he was the author of the incident. "It was I who did it. I was betrayed by the cameras. I'm so sorry. It's my worst nightmare. I was watching the video again and again and still do not understand how this could happen. My mother tells me it was not my fault and that's what I want to believe; the referee should never have conceded the goal. I just hope the fans really understand and forgive me," the teenager apologized. A real own goal.

LONG DISTANCE

On September 25, 2011, striker Jone Samuelsen broke a very strange record: He scored the farthest goal scored from a header in a first division match in the world. Samuelsen, from the Norwegian club Odd Greenland BK, defeated Mostafa Abdellaoue of Tromsø IL with a headshot 60 yards from the rival goal at Skagerak Arena. In truth, Abdellaoue was not exactly protecting his goal, since he had gone up to look for the tie in a corner kick in the last minute of the match that his team lost 2 to 1. The corner kick was rejected by the host's defense, and the last man from Tromsø tried to swing the ball toward the Odd Greenland area. But it fell short and Samuelsen, with a header from his own field to the side of the center circle, sent the ball to the unprotected visitors' goal, where it entered with a smooth roll to put the final 3-1.

A month later, a daring defender of the Japanese team Fagiano Okayama FC broke the Norwegian's record by 3 feet, although in a match for the Second Division. Ryujiro Ueda, defender of Fagiano, headed the ball in his half of field—also next to the central circle, although to the left—after a long goal kick by the Yokohama FC's goalie, Kentro Seki. After the header, the ball overtook Seki, who had inexplicably come to the edge of his area. The weak keeper tried to recover but couldn't avoid the goal or erase his name from the *Guinness Book of World Records*.

APOCRYPHAL RESULTS

The reactions of the fans in the face of an adverse result have generated an innumerable amount of real hells inside soccer stadiums. In order to stop a pressure cooker explosion and to protect their lives, those of their fans and those of the soccer players, many referees have resorted to an unusual containment mechanism: simulation. In fields all around the world, it's happened that a referee, usually with the participation of the players as co-stars, mounted an improvised play to make the spectators believe that their team tied or won and thus upset the mood of the people, although in fact the "official" match had already been suspended. Probably, the most famous of these performances occurred on August 2, 1962, at the Urbano Caldeira stadium in Santos FC, where the local squad faced CA Peñarol in the rematch of the final of the Copa Libertadores in 1962. The team that was led by Pelé had won in Uruguay in the legendary Centenario of Montevideo, 1-2, and with a draw at home would secure their first continental title. In fact, after the halftime whistle, Santos was up on the scoreboard, 2-1, but in the second half the Uruguayans brought out their well-earned badge of honor acquired in the Maracanazo of the 1950 Brazil World Cup, to turn the scoreboard by the goals of the Ecuadorian Alberto Spencer (at 49 minutes) and José "Pepe" Sasía (at 51). The partial victory left the Brazilian fans outraged, who began throwing all kinds of projectiles onto the pitch. In a corner kick, a bottle knocked out Chilean referee Carlos Robles. In the report that he later submitted to CONMEBOL, the referee explained: "Seven minutes passed from the start of the second half, and I had called a corner kick in favor of the Santos team. When I got near the sideline, a bottle was thrown at me. Because of this I was knocked semi-unconscious and momentarily blinded, and when I regained my lucidity, I found myself in the dressing room surrounded by the Santos officials, so I decided to suspend the match because I did not have any guarantees to develop my mission; the Brazilian directors tried to convince me to continue the game, which I flatly refused. Due to my attitude, I was threatened by the president of the São Paulo Federation, João Mendonça Falcão, who told me that if I did not continue directing the match, he, as a deputy, would have me detained by the police. As I stood firm by my decision, he insulted me in front of my colleagues, (Sergio) Bustamante and (Domingo) Massaro, telling me 'thief, coward, I can prove that you are a scoundrel.' Two other people who had entered the dressing room under the pretense to change my attitude, Luis Alonso, Santos coach, and club president, Athie Jorge Coury, insulted me and said that they did not answer for my life when leaving the stadium."

Peñarol's men also received a shower of objects—stones, beer glass containers—and death threats from spectators, rivals, and even some police officers who supposedly had to protect them. In this dangerous context, Robles took out the ace of spades from his deck of cards that would allow him to return home safe and sound. After a suspension of 51 minutes, the referee returned to the field and met in the middle of the field with the Uruguayans Sasía, Néstor Gonçalves and goalkeeper Luis Maidana and confessed that the game was already suspended but that it would play the remaining 39 minutes to defuse the situation. "Guys, help me out here, because if not, they'll kill us all," the ref pleaded.

In a few minutes Santos "tied" through their striker Pagão. The men of Peñarol almost did not step on the rival penalty box, a fact that went unnoticed for fans, players, and leaders of the team from São Paulo, which after the final whistle unleashed an exorbitant celebration. None, not even journalists, learned about the staging. In fact, newspapers like *O Estado* titled in their editions the following day "Santos tied: they are America's champions."

The bucket of cold water came hours later when CONMEBOL announced the annulment of the draw, ratified the Peñarol victory, and ordered both clubs to meet in a third and final duel in Buenos Aires four weeks later, refereed by the prestigious Dutch ref, Leo Horn. On September 30, in the "Monumental" of River Plate, Santos crushed Peñarol 3-0 with two goals from Pele and another own goal by defender Omar Caetano. The Brazilians finally had their longed-for trophy. The Uruguayan players, like the Chilean Robles, at least lived to tell the tale.

A Dutch referee, Laurens Van Ravens, was also responsible for another empty celebration, although for a very different situation that had nothing to do with violence. Van Ravens was appointed by UEFA for the return fixture of the 1971/72 European Cup Winners' Cup between Sporting Clube de Portugal and Rangers FC of Scotland. The first game had ended 3-2 for the Scots, and in the Portuguese capital the score was repeated in favor of the Lusitanians after 90 minutes of intense fighting. As indicated in the regulation, the referee played an extra half hour, divided into two 15-minute segments. In that period, both teams scored a goal, which raised the overall score to 6-6. Van Ravens, then, used a brand-new tiebreaker system incorporated into international competitions: a series of shots from the penalty spot. In that instance, the agile local keeper Vitor Damas kept his goal unbeaten—he saved three shots and a fourth was kicked out—for Sporting to prevail 2-0. The euphoria that gripped the stands of the Alvalade stadium lasted only a little while: when the referee entered his locker room, a UEFA delegate informed him that the winner was Rangers because, by scoring during the extra time, they added more away goals than the Portuguese squad. The Dutchman, embarrassed, had to explain his mistake in both dressing rooms and then went to the press room to immolate himself before the cameras and microphones, recognizing that the victory was, in truth, defeat, and vice versa. The Scottish, revitalized, beat Torino FC in the quarterfinals, FC Bayern München in the semifinals, and, in the climactic match played on May 24, 1972, at FC Barcelona's Camp Nou, FC Dinamo Moscow.

AN UNENDING GALE

It is said that man proposes but God disposes. And, sometimes, man wants to play soccer but God (or nature, according to agnostics or atheists) determines that the ball will not walk on water, freeze over snow, or fly, not due to a kick, but by the mercy of tornadoes and storms generated by Aeolus. Thousands of drenched soccer days suffered suspensions and postponements, and others weathered the storm with unusual measures.

On January 18, 1879, the day in which the England and Wales teams played their first official match, an unending storm urged the captains to agree on a "short" match of two 30-minute halves, which was welcomed by the drenched English head referee Segard Bastard. The match was held at the Oval Stadium in the London neighborhood of Kennington, where the home squad won 2-1 despite playing the first twenty minutes with ten men, since midfielder William Clegg arrived late to the English capital because the train he had taken in Sheffield, had been delayed by the bad weather.

GONE WITH THE WATER

A storm may not be enough reason to stop the ball rolling, but there is always room for a scandal over water. In November 2003, in Turkey, the rain accompanied the ninety minutes of the first division clash between Fenerbahçe Spor Kulübü and Çaykur Rizespor Kulübü, guided by the alert performance of referee Ali Aydin. Well, not so alert, because Aydin twice warned Rizespor's Colombian defender, Gustavo Victoria, but, the man having a bit of memory issues, did not show him the red card. The match ended 1-1 and provoked a shower...of complaints from the Fenerbahçe managers. After a lawsuit was filed to have the result reviewed, the Federation summoned the referee to explain the error. Aydin explained that he had not thrown out Victoria because the first warning, duly noted on the yellow card, had been erased by the water falling. What he didn't clarify was how he had forgotten the first yellow. After analyzing what happened, the association ordered the replay of the match on January 18. Fenerbahçe prevailed 4-1, and that triumph, at the end of the season, allowed them to be crowned champions.

LIGHTNING!

It is not easy to explain what happened in the Democratic Republic of the Congo in October 1998. In the province of Kasai, the teams from two villages, Bena Tshadi and Basangana, faced each other under a leaden sky that threatened a strong storm. In the middle of the match, the storm began, and lightning struck the field. The violent volley immediately and tragically killed the eleven local players, but unbelievably did not affect any of Basangana's men. In an attempt to clarify what happened, the local newspaper *L'Avenir* evaluated that the phenomenon could be the work of a sorcerer, especially because the twenty-two protagonists and the referee were scattered and mixed throughout the field.

SCORERS IN THE FOG

Fog is one of the worst enemies of soccer. When a dense cloud gets into a stadium, confusion and darkness reigns. If you can't see, the game can't continue. Although some, like Richard Siddall, didn't realize that. On September 12, 2003, in the English county of Cheshire, near Sheffield, Witton Albion FC and Stocksbridge Park Steels FC were ten minutes into the match for the Northern Premier Football League, a semi-professional division, when a thick fog arose that forced the match to be suspended. A while later, in the changing rooms, the Stocksbridge Steels coach Wayne Biggins noticed the absence of keeper Siddall and went to look for him. The goalkeeper was "focused" on the match under the goalposts. When Biggins informed the "1" that the game had been suspended for several minutes, Siddall turned red as a tomato and admitted that he "was waiting for a rival striker to appear in the mist." The poor goalie was received in the locker room by a rain of laughter from his companions. He was not the only one to suffer this embarrassment. Sam Bartram, keeper for Charlton Athletic FC, was also left alone when his club visited Chelsea FC in the capital at Stamford Bridge on December 25, 1937, for the English tournament. The city of London is famous for its massive fog, and surely Bartram would still be at his goal if a policeman had not warned him that the game had been suspended for almost half an hour.

The game was 73 minutes in when a sudden haze forced the referee to whistle the end of the match between Oldham Athletic AFC 2 and Brentford FC 1 for the third round of the FA English Cup on January 8, 1927. With fast reflexes, the visiting coach, Harry Curtis, sent his boys straight to the showers with the excuse of rushing to run to the train station and travel the nearly 160 miles that separated them from home from Boundary Park, in Greater Manchester, to the London suburb of Brentford. The regulation of the FA Cup indicated that any game canceled by circumstances beyond its normal development should start with the score and the chronometer blank, and the astute coach Curtis knew this well. As if it had been foreseen, the cloud broke up as quickly as it arrived, and the referee called the teams to resume action. Curtis refused, maintaining that his boys were already bathed and saying that putting on shirts drenched in sweat again could cause pneumonia. The ref hesitated, but, finally, he accepted the approach of the away coach and the match was then canceled and rescheduled "from scratch" for two days later. On January 10, Brentford's team returned to Boundary Park...to take a resounding 2-4 victory.

When he visited Moscow in May 1945, before the start of the Cold War, Clementine Ogilvy Spencer, the wife of British Prime Minister Winston Churchill, thought it was an excellent idea for FC Dinamo Moscow to tour the United Kingdom to strengthen the then cordial ties between both nations. The Soviet team accepted the invitation and traveled to participate in several friendly matches, including one with Arsenal FC in London but at the home of Tottenham Hotspur FC, White Hart Lane. That November 21, the English squad was prevailing 3-2, until a haze settled on the pitch, and, although it didn't completely limit vision, it obscured the normal development of the game and the task of the Russian referee Nikolai Latychev. In the second half, Dinamo managed to turn the score to win 3-4. Several journalists and historians assert that the away team took advantage of the circumstances to make several "changes" without removing the replaced and, thus, win the match with between 13 and 15 players against "just" 11 of the English players. This version of events was never officially confirmed, but that feeds the long rumor mill of soccer.

In the art of taking advantage of climatic issues to the max, nobody has surpassed the Catalan coach Xavi Agustí. In 1972, when he managed the Club Deportiu Banyoles in the Spanish fourth division, Agustí traveled with his players from the city of Banyoles to neighboring Olot to face Unió Esportiva Olot. When they arrived, the manager noticed that a fog covered the Municipal Estadi and did not allow them to see beyond 30 to 40 feet. Agustí asked the referee to postpone the game, but he, instead, haughtily rejected the observation of the visiting manager: "Here, I command." The coach was left with subdued, but promised to teach the arrogant referee a lesson. As soon as the match started, he sent all his substitutes to warm up behind Olot's goal with one mission: in each corner shot, one or two of them had to get into the area and mix with their companions, protected by the cloudy curtain. Banyoles won that day 0-1 with a header after a corner kick scored by a "ghost" player who "disappeared" from the field after starters and substitutes celebrated the goal in a huge embrace. But the matter didn't end there: Before the end, Agustí ordered one of the substitutes to stay on the field until the match ended. When the referee called the end of the match, the coach approached him and asked him to count the players for the away team. The referee was stunned to count twelve men from Banyoles on the field. "Do you see why you couldn't play the game in these conditions?" he ironically asked. The lesson had been learned.

THE KING'S STORY

Though this story also has to do with a whimsical fog, it still deserves a prominent place in soccer history for its unique context, its incredible development, and its fantastic end. On January 1, 1940, four months after the British King George VI declared war on Germany and Adolf Hitler, the Scottish clubs Hibernian FC and Hearts of Midlothian FC met on Easter Road to play a new Edinburgh derby with 14,000 people on hand to watch. The match, and its radio transmission, was authorized to distract the nervous population a bit, but the fear of an attack by the Luftwaffe, the Nazi air force, forced them to take some measures. Although the Scottish capital was covered by thick clouds that afternoon, the British Broadcasting Corporation (BBC) management bluntly ordered the journalist Bob Kingsley to remark several times during the match that it was being played under a radiant sun. The idea for this was that, if an eventual German spy listened to the signal, he could not direct an air attack against Edinburgh. Kingsley accepted and prepared to deploy all his skills in order to describe the actions of the sports duel and, at the same time, cheat enemies with his comments on the weather. He never imagined that his effort would be so superb. Seconds before the start of the derby, the clouds descended and formed into a thick fog that blinded the fans, the players, the referee, and Kingsley himself. The journalist, who couldn't see ten past the edge of his nose, not only had to invent the weather also had to call a completely fictitious match. Passes, shots, saves, fouls, and nonexistent goals were described one after another with exceptional detail under a sky as clear as glass. The public saw as little as he did, and the players could not conduct two passes in a row. So invisible was what was happening on the other side of the end line, that Kingsley, on the verge of dysphonia and a nervous breakdown, did not know that the game was over and extended his narrative ten minutes beyond the final whistle. On top of that, his "passionate 3-3 draw" had been, in fact, an electrifying victory for Hearts 6-5. It is often said that soccer announcers say a lot of nonsense. Surely none can compete with Kingsley's work that day. But, in his favor, it should be noted that he did it for a valiant cause.

AN INFAMOUS HAZE

Everton FC was manhandling Woolwich Arsenal FC (today simply called Arsenal FC) at the London-based Manor Ground on November 26, 1904. The "Toffees" (as this club in the city of Liverpool is known because close to the place where their home was established, Goodison Park, there was a famous candy store) was comfortably winning 1-3 and climbed to the top of the English First Division tournament. However, the victory was not won because, just 14 minutes from the end, the traditional and compact fog of the British capital suddenly appeared to cover the entire playing field with its opaque cloak. The referee suspended the play, and a few days later the Football Association ruled that the match would be played again "from the beginning." Everton protested the decision, even more when it was determined that this match was intercalated at the end of the season between two other duels against Manchester City FC and Nottingham Forest FC with an aggravating factor: The Toffees had to face three duels in four days, all away. Despite the complaints, Everton showed up to play each match. On Friday, April 21, they fell 2-0 in Manchester; the next day, they returned to London to change their 1-3 win by a 2-1 defeat with Woolwich Arsenal, this time under the shining sun; on Monday 24, the squad from Liverpool defeated Nottingham Forest 0-2, but this victory was not enough to win the title, which went to Newcastle United by only a one-point difference!

THE SINGER

By 1906, AC Milan signed a Dutch goalie named François Knoote, who also excelled as a singer and had performed successfully at the Metropolitan Opera in New York. For the quality of his performance under the goalposts, Knoote was considered the team's goalkeeper although he had a curious rule: He only trained or played on the days without rain and when the dry was ground to take care of his throat and prevent against a possible cold that would affect his career as a singer. His greatest desire was to participate in an opera at the famous Teatro Alla Scala in Milan. On Friday, when the players met to assemble the team for Sunday, Knoote first went through the Vittorio Emanuele II gallery, situated in the center of the city, in front of the Duomo, where there was a barometer that forecasted eventual storms. If the instrument predicted bad weather (something relatively common in the populous Lombard capital), the Dutch player left his position to the substitute goalkeeper, Attilio Trere. One afternoon, while Milan was playing on their old field with Knoote in the goal, a "passing" cloud suddenly covered the sky and unleashed a brief downpour. In the middle of a play, the Milanese players realized that their goal had been empty. The goalkeeper had taken refuge from the drops in the locker room! Milan continued the match with ten men, one of them in the abandoned position, and Knoote only returned to the field when the sky cleared and the sun shone again.

TURNED WITH THE WIND

The goal that FC Dinamo Kyiv scored against Maccabi Haifa FC on February 29, 2012, was definitely unique. Both teams played a friendly in the sports village of the Israeli institution—in the middle of a gale. The wind, which blew very hard, seemed to complicate the home team more, since they lost 0-4 in 60 minutes of play. At that moment, the host goalkeeper, Assaf Mendes, cut off a Ukrainian cross and threw the ball to the ground to take a powerful and high kick into the rival midfield. But a violent burst of wind crossed his path and "kicked" the ball toward the Israeli goal with unusual hardness. The ball made a lively meandering path, sticking to the right side of the Maccabi goal with poor Mendes being unable to react and avoid his unusual own goal. Both the Dinamo boys and the referee expressed their solidarity with the goalkeeper: the former did not celebrate the goal, and the referee immediately suspended the match.

A 14-YEAR-OLD LINE JUDGE

Two minutes before the meeting that took place on April 28, 1991, between CA Huracán and CA Chaco For Ever, for the Argentine first division, a voice came over the loudspeakers of the Buenos Aires stadium Tomás Adolfo Ducó, urging: "If any AFA licensed referee is in the stands, we urgently request your presence in the dressing room." It so happened that one of the line judges who had to assist Guillermo Marconi, Oscar Pesce, had not arrived in time for the match, so they had to resort to an improvised replacement. But, as none of those present responded to the call, Marconi, very riskily, handed the flag to a 14-year-old teenager who had gone to the stadium to witness the match... as a fan of Huracán! The boy, Leonardo Fernández Blanco, was encouraged and, although he did not wear a black uniform, collaborated with the referee to start the game. The young man's task only extended to 28 minutes of the first half, when he was replaced by the late Pesce. "Marconi gave me only one indication: to raise the flag for the side-outs," said Fernandez Blanco at the end of the match. The referee, meanwhile, explained that his decision was still within regulations. That afternoon, Huracán defeated the Chaco team 4-3, but the work of the boy, confessed a Huracán fan, did not favor the local team at all. In fact, at the time of his "substitution," the score was 1-1.

FLAG BY MICROPHONE

Almost as bizarre as the previous case was a situation in England. On September 16, 1972, shortly after the end of the first half of a momentous Arsenal FC versus Liverpool FC match, one of the line judges, Dennis Drewitt, made a bad move and pulled a muscle. Drewitt held until the 45 minutes were completed but gave up continuing because of the severity of the injury and the intense pain he felt. In those times, matches did not have a fourth referee, so that, by loudspeakers, a call was made to the large audience sitting in the Highbury stands (about 45,000 people) to see if there was a qualified referee to fill the vacancy during second half. As no one showed up, referee Pat Partridge decided to suspend the match, which was broadcasted live on television. This piece of data is important: to avoid that the game was suspended and have the viewers left without their scheduled program, the TV commentator Jimmy Hill offered to take the flag. Years before he had become a sports journalist, Jimmy had completed the rigorous referee accreditation class. Hill offered his help to Partridge. "If you do not find another person better qualified, I'll help you with pleasure; it's a shame that the game should be interrupted," the commentator told the referee. Dressed in a gray suit, black shirt, pink tie, and shoes, Hill went down to one of the dressing rooms, where he was provided with sneakers and a light-blue sports outfit, more appropriate to exercise his new function. The show could go on. The duel ended without goals, which favored Liverpool. A few dates later they were crowned champions with three points advantage over Arsenal.

YOU DON'T COME OUT!

Fábio Baiano couldn't stand it anymore. Thanks to a strain causing intense pain in the left thigh and forcing him to limp, the Sport Club Corinthians Paulista offensive midfielder decided to leave the field. But when he approached the sideline by the substitutes' bench at the Pacaembu stadium in the Brazilian city of San Pablo, the Timao's coach, Tite, came out to meet him: "No, no, you don't leave, you stay on the field," the coach ordered. That day, September 26, 2004, Corinthians, who was tied goalless with Goiás Esporte Clube for the Brazilian championship's first division, had already made the three changes authorized by the rules and couldn't afford to stay with a man down when there were still 15 minutes left, as they needed a victory that would bring them closer to qualify for the Copa Libertadores. However, Baiano, in lots of pain, did not want to listen to Tite. Player and coach, then, engaged in a heated argument while the game continued. "I'm staying, but I'm not thinking of moving," the player said, reluctantly. But his love for the game was stronger and at 89 minutes, when a pass found him alone in the midfield, Baiano reacted and ran at full speed to the rival penalty box and, when he was met by the only defender who was in the visiting team's rearguard, pulled a tremendous right shot that, after flying 25 meters, hit the crossbar, came down inside the goal, and went to rest in the net. The scorer ran to embrace Tite and greeted him with an indulgent "you were right." Corinthians got an emotional 1-0 victory that, although it was not enough to qualify for the Libertadores, allowed the Paulista team to access the Copa Sudamericana.

SOLIDARITY

On November 7, 2004, during an Italian Serie A match played at the Atleti Azzurri d'Italia stadium, Unione Calcio Sampdoria forward Fabio Bazzani jumped to head the ball and accidentally nudged Cesare Natali, from rival Atalanta Bergamasca Calcio, in the face. The collision opened a deep and bloody wound on Natali's face, who had to be assisted by doctors to the sideline. To the surprise of the spectators, the referees, and the rest of the players, Bazzani, instead of continuing playing, waited outside the field for his colleague to recover and only returned to the game three minutes later, together with the injured defender. The chivalrous attitude was highly praised by the fans and the press, although Bazzani played down his decent action. "I'm not a saint. I do not feel like I'm a saint, because many times soccer brings out the worst side, but there are unwritten codes, and loyalty and respect for the opponent are not as strange as it may seem from the outside," said the player. Natali, however, was grateful for the gesture: "Fabio behaved superbly. I think he was a bit afraid to see me bleed so much, he hit me with his elbow to defend the ball, but it was unintentional. It was a great way to apologize." The match ended in a draw, but the spectators enjoyed Bazzani's attitude and fair play.

WHITE FLAG

The biggest win of the Argentine superclásico Boca Juniors-River Plate, one of the matches between the most colorful and passionate clubs of the world, took place during the Amateur Era, on December 23, 1928, in a very strange match of the former first division of Argentina. Boca was the superior team from the starting whistle and opened the score after three minutes with an effective kick by Domingo Tarasconi. This bucket of cold water woke up River, who went hurriedly in search of the equalizer, and a few minutes later, at 20 minutes, got a corner kick that seemed promising. Manuel Debatte launched a cross from the corner flag, and two "millionaire" players, Gerónimo Uriarte and Alejandro Giglio, went high up to get the ball. But, instead of the ball, the two men head-butted each other and were both knocked out, suffering from severe concussions. River continued with nine men—at that time substitutions were not allowed—and Boca didn't let the train pass: Esteban Kuko and Roberto Cherro scored a double each to raise the score to 5-0. According to the newspaper *La Nación,* ten minutes from the end, another player for the Millionaires, Francisco Gondar, had to be taken off, having fainted after receiving a powerful ball in the stomach. River was thus 8 against 11 on the pitch and 0-5 on the scoreboard. In the next play, Tarasconi was left alone before the goalkeeper Carlos Isola, who remained motionless and did not resist for the sixth goal, in supposed disagreement due to the abysmal difference. With his team dead on the field and the score, the River Plate

123

captain, Camilo Bonelli, asked the referee Eduardo Forte for mercy, and he granted it when there was still about eight minutes left to play. Boca got an overwhelming 6-0 victory, never equaled or tied in the history of the Superclásico, and the only reason the score difference wasn't wider was because River deployed the white flag!

LION HEART

Harry Lyon earned the status "legendary hero" of English club Wigan Athletic FC in an incredible match played in Springfield Park against Doncaster Rovers FC on November 17, 1965. That day, both teams met again to unlock a draw at two for the first-round FA Cup, which took place four days earlier at Belle Vue, the old stadium of the Doncaster Rovers. The story started very bad for Wigan: the away team opened the score almost immediately and Lyon, star attacker, left the field on a stretcher at 19 minutes after receiving a terrible kick in the left ankle, which the 7,000 spectators thought was broken. However, in the dressing room, a doctor checked Lyon and noted that there was no fracture, but the ligaments were really damaged and there was a giant hematoma. However, Lyon's heart was bigger than the inflammation: He ordered the physician to tightly bandage the injury and to give him aspirin, which he washed down...with whiskey! After halftime and dozens of kisses for the bottle of tasty Scottish liquor, Lyon, revitalized by the powerful cocktail of painkillers and alcohol, returned with new vigor to the field. His performance was fantastic: He scored the three goals that gave Wigan the victory and the pass to the next round of the Cup. Two were scored with the injured leg. The home fans celebrated the extraordinary feat, which the idol himself couldn't celebrate; the vapors of alcohol had clouded the head of Lyon, who was on the field in body, but not in soul. After a long shower in the locker room, the scorer came back from his drunkenness and admitted to his excited teammates that he did not remember a single detail of his incredible deed.

HAT TRICK

For a central defender to score a hat trick is rare, but even stranger was the case of a West Ham United FC defender, Alvin Martin, who on April 21, 1986, against Newcastle United for the English first division, got a hat trick against three different goalkeepers! But how could such a situation happen? Even at the expense of injuries?

That afternoon, at London's Upton Park, Martin pushed a cross by Alan Devonshire from the left and broke the resistance of Welsh goalkeeper Martin Thomas. In the second half, already with the score 4-0, Thomas collided with a local forward and hurt his right shoulder. He could not continue, and he was replaced by the only substitute authorized at that time by the Football Association, the midfielder Ian Stewart, but the green jersey was put on by midfielder Chris Hedworth. Martin returned to the penalty area to head into the net a corner kick from the right thrown by Mark Ward, who beat the hands of Hedworth and increased the score to 5 for the home squad. In his attempt to prevent the goal, the improvised goalkeeper collided against his right post and fractured his collarbone, so he also had to leave the field. This time without substitutions, Newcastle was playing with ten men and its striker Peter Beardsley under the goalposts. Six minutes from the end and with the score 7-1, Glenn Roeder from the away team committed a rough foul on the attacker Tony Cottee inside the penalty area, which led to a logical penalty. The Scottish defender Ray Stewart was in charge of firing from the twelve yards but gave the opportunity to Martin because his name was on the mouth of all the fans, who wanted to see him score the hat trick. With a right cross, Martin got the eighth goal of West Ham and completed this unusual triple score before a hat-trick of goalkeepers.

HIRSCHL'S INSTRUCTIONS

To prepare for the 1938 championship, CA River Plate hired Emérico Hirschl, an angry Hungarian who was known for treating his players very badly. However, despite this peculiar quality of the European, which was not seen favorably by soccer players, his grumblings paid off more than once. On the afternoon of August 7 of that year, for the 15th round of the first division tournament, the coach of the "millionaire" team was having difficulty putting together the squad to face Racing Club in Avellaneda. Hirschl, who was struggling because several of the players were injured, saw that in one of the stands was sitting one of them, Luis María Rongo, a great forward who suffered from a muscular ailment. The coach summoned the attacker to the dressing room through the loudspeakers of the stadium and, when the attacker showed up, threw a shirt at him and ordered him: "Play and win, because, if not, I'll break your head." "Motivated" by the tactical instruction of the Hungarian, Rongo went out on the field and, in spite of the injury, scored the three goals with which the squad of the red band defeated the Academy, 2-3.

LOUD AND RUDE

Manchester United FC goalkeeper Alex Stepney was in a very bad mood on August 19, 1975. As the first division match against Birmingham City FC in St. Andrews began, the "1" from the away team started spewing loud shouts to his defenders. More irascible than ever, Stepney ranted again and again with loud vociferations and disgusting insults. Suddenly, as if by magic, the goalie stopped emitting the fiery sounds that his teammates were long since tired of hearing. The Manchester players thought that Stepney had come to his senses and modified his sullen character that afternoon. Far from it! The goalie had dislocated his jaw from so much screaming! After being assisted by a doctor, the screamer, very sore, had to leave the field. Without a chance to make a substitution, his place was occupied by the midfielder Brian Greenhoff, and the visiting squad completed the match with ten players, which was no obstacle to beating Birmingham 0-2.

THE DIAGNOSIS

In May of 1929, in a very close game between CA Huracán, the leader of the Argentine amateur first division tournament, and CA Independiente, was playing at Huracán's home of Parque de los Patricios. The visiting goalkeeper Néstor Sangiovanni collided with an Huracán striker and was knocked down for several minutes. At that time, the usual thing was for the home club to provide a doctor for the 22 protagonists. So basically, the Independiente goalkeeper, principally responsible for the scorecard being blank, was being examined by a Huracán fan. The rogue doctor, seeing an opportunity to help his team being served to him on a platter, put his passion before the Hippocratic Oath. He said that Sangiovanni had three fractured ribs and called an ambulance to take the "1" to a nearby hospital. The goal, then, was covered by defender Ernesto Chiarella, and the Avellaneda's team continued with ten men. Despite the ruse, the numerical advantage obtained by the malicious doctor did not stop Independiente from defeating Huracán 1-2. Failing in his stratagem, the doctor finally acknowledged his "error" to the visiting officers and admitted that Sangiovanni had not suffered a fracture, but only had a strong bruise. At least, he did not slip them an invoice for his services.

THE DECEIVER

The French book *Les incroyables du football* ensures us that, in the 1930s, the French team FC Sochaux-Montbéliard had in its ranks an English forward named Cropper, who wore dentures. The journalist Sylvie Lauduique-Hamez tells us that, during a league match, Cropper entered the rival penalty box and, after a slight contact with a defender, dropped down in a spectacular manner. While the Briton landed on the grass, he spat out the prosthesis. The referee, seeing the teeth on the ground, believed that the blow had been brutal and marked a penalty kick for Sochaux. Thanks to this trick, "the puppies" (as this squad located in the east of France, very close to Switzerland, founded by the Peugeot family as a recreational activity for their employees, is known) won the match and Cropper two Oscar awards: one for the best performance, and another for the best special effects.

HALFTIME

The halftime is a period of rest and recovery between the two halves of a soccer game—a moment in which nothing happens on the field, but that usually results in very heated situations in the locker rooms, ideal for breaking deals. In 2003, Iraty Sport Club, a team from the Brazilian state league of Paraná, went to their locker rooms at home with a 1-4 score against Prudentópolis Esporte Clube. Their anxious president, Sergio Malucelli, did not want to wait until the end of the game to unload his anger caused by the humiliating beating. As soon as the first half was over, he went down to the locker room and fired Marco Antonio, the goalkeeper of the team, right then and there.

Another person who "took advantage" of the period of supposed rest to give free rein to his fury was the Argentine coach Néstor Clausen. In October 2006, the former defender—World Champion in Mexico in 1986—resigned his position at Football Club Sion in the middle of a match that his team, leader of the Swiss Super League first division, lost 0-1 to FC La Chaux de Fonds, of the second division, for the Helvetic national Cup. Clausen argued that his players did not support him. The final result of that match seemed to be right: Sion won 3 to 1.

In 1999, the president of the German team Sport Club Fortuna Köln, a bad-tempered millionaire named Jean Löring, fired his coach, former international goalkeeper Harald "Toni"

Schumacher, at halftime of a second division match while losing 0- 2 against SV Waldhof Mannheim. Schumacher immediately left the Südstadion and went home to watch the match on television and enjoy how his former team, led by Löring himself, lost 1-5.

RESISTING TEMPTATION

Cameroon must be stopped, no matter what. As a defender of the 2000 title, the "indomitable lions" were the favorites to keep the 2002 African Cup of Nations, which was being held again in Mali. On February 7, Cameroon had to face the host squad in the semifinal. This alarmed the Malian leaders, who recognized the rival's superiority. After a quick review of the situation, the managers decided to resort to an extra-sportive stratagem that would help them achieve victory on the field: filling the hotel in Bamako, the Malian capital where the Cameroonians stayed, with young and beautiful prostitutes. However, the visiting soccer players resisted temptation and remained deaf to the sweet song of the beautiful "sirens" who wanted to reduce their strength with their lovemaking virtues. Cameroon crushed the home side 3-0, and in the final defeated Senegal with penalties. It is not known whether, once the Olympic lap ended, the champions evaluated loosening their resistance and succumbing to the charms of the ladies. Anyway, the hotel was surprisingly "empty" just after the semifinal.

WHY DID YOU COMPLAIN?

The 1993/94 campaign of the German club FC Nürnberg Verein für Leibesübungen was bad enough for its own officials to intervene, exchanging an injustice for a tragedy. On April 23, 1994, the Bavarian squad traveled to nearby Munich to face the giant FC Bayern München at its Olympic stadium. With the score 1-0, a corner from the right for the home team fell on the feet of defender Thomas Helmer, who under the crossbar and a couple of inches from the goal line pushed the ball out! The tremendous error of the Munich defender was followed by another much worse by referee Hans-Joachim Osmers and his assistant Jörg Jablonski, who, incredibly, gave a "goal" to the home side. The Nürnberg players complained, but their argument fell on deaf ears. Osmers remained firm, and the match continued as usual. The visitors finally fell 2-1, and their leaders ran to the headquarters of the German federation with a video of the match that clearly showed that the ball driven by Helmer had not crossed the goal line. It was an unobjectionable "ghost goal." After analyzing the situation, the entity gave in to the complaint of the representatives of Nürnberg and ordered that the game be replayed. The two clubs returned to the Olympic stadium on May 3, and this time referee Bernd Heynemann was assigned to oversee the match. Bayern München prevailed in this second opportunity by 5 to 0, relegating their rivals! The directors of Nürnberg never again protested a match.

DOUBLE RELEGATION

When they came out on the pitch on April 20, 2002, CA Platense and CA Racing de Córdoba had one objective in common: to win to stay in the National B, the second Argentine Division. A defeat meant relegation; a draw would make them depend on other results. The duel ended 2-2 with goals from Diego Graieb and Luis Velázquez for the host team of Platense and from José Luis Fernández and Carlos Bertola from the penalty spot for the Córdoba club. As there were also two draws in the matches of the other clubs committed to saving their place in the division (Godoy Cruz Antonio Tomba and El Porvenir), Platense and Racing together went down together. A double relegation.

FATAL HAT TRICKS

CA Boca Juniors and CA San Lorenzo de Almagro met for the first time in the first division on November 7, 1915, Boca's field at that time in the Buenos Aires town of Wilde, Avellaneda. That inaugural edition of which, years later, would be one of the most important derbies of Argentine soccer, had the visiting player José Coll as the top scorer of the afternoon with three goals. Unfortunately for Coll, who played as a goalie, that meant five balls got past him.

At 30 minutes during the first half, with the scoreboard blank, a powerful cross sent by the local striker Luis Ruggiero, who made his debut that same day, went past the goalkeeper into the net. Already in the second half, with Boca up 3-0—the forwards Adolfo Taggino and Antonio Galeano had increased the score at 35 and 42 minutes, respectively—the goalkeeper went out to cut a new advance by their rivals but, after a series of rebounds that culminated in bouncing off one of his legs, the ball ended up in the net. Minutes later, extremely disturbed by his disastrous performance, Coll caught the ball and sent it straight to the back of the goal, which determined the fifth and final goal of the match that served as the kickoff to the traditional duel between Boca and San Lorenzo.

One of the most bizarre encounters in the Bundesliga occurred on December 14, 2009, when Borussia VFL 1900 Mönchengladbach faced Hannoverscher Sportverein von 1896. That afternoon, in Borussia Park, there was a cataract of goals: the Tunisian Karim Haggui, of the visiting team, opened the scoreboard; then the Canadian Rob Friend (Borussia) scored, followed by the Ivorians Didier Ya Konan and Constant Djapka (Hannover), the American Michael Bradley (for the hosts), Ya Konan again, the German Christian Schulz (Hannover), and finally the Tunisian scored again. If you read it like that, Hannover won by a landslide, 2-6. However, the two goals by Haggui and Djapka were own goals, so Borussia won the match 5-3. The Deutscher Fußball-Bund (the German Football Federation) started an investigation to determine if any abnormality had occurred in that match, such as a bribe or some arrangement linked to the mafias of illegal gambling. The only conclusion that was reached was that Haggui's and Djapka's play had been the result of their own clumsiness only.

Another calamity equivalent was suffered by the players and fans of Sheffield Wednesday FC on December 26, 1952. Players from the central England team scored seven goals, but still fell 4-5 to West Bromwich Albion, which benefited from the generous hat trick.

According to the "history books," at a professional level, there would only be three "field" players (to exempt the aforementioned goalkeeper José Coll) responsible for an embarrassing hat trick in their own goal in first division: one is the Argentine Jorge Ninjo, who with his bad aim helped Clube Atlético Mineiro defeat Esporte Clube Democrata 5-1 for the 1982 Minas Gerais state championship.

Equally dishonorable, although more frustrating, is the case of Belgian Stan Van den Buys of the late club Germinal Ekeren FC (in 1999 it merged with another squad, Beerschot AC, to form Koninklijke Beerschot Antwerpen Club). On January 22, 1995, Van den Buys contributed his hat trick to have his team fall to Anderlecht...2-3! In short, the squad of Antwerp lost although the five goals of the match were the work of their own men.

In 1958, in the Colombian city of Manizales, Club Atlético Bucaramanga was winning 3-4 against the home team, Deportes Caldas (today Once Caldas). The three scores of the home squad had been obtained by the same player, Orlando "Popcorn" Martínez, who was wearing the shirt of...Bucaramanga! Just one minute from the end, the referee called for a corner kick for Caldas. Upon learning that his teammates were distributed in a disorderly manner in the penalty box to reject the Caldas attack, the Argentine striker Miguel Zazzini ran to them and, screaming, ordered his defenders: "Please, take Popcorn!!" With Martinez well contained, Bucaramanga managed to maintain the victory despite the disappointing play.

A STRIKE AGAINST HIS OWN GOAL

The match was ending. That afternoon, December 17, 1955, Blackpool FC had been trounced in Highbury, the stronghold of London's powerful Arsenal FC. Jimmy Bloomfield, Vic Groves, Cliff Holton, and Derek Tapscott had scored the goals for a 4-0 beating that was about to conclude. In those last moments, the skillful host defender Denis Evans recovered a ball almost at half field and, by effect of the play, faced his goalkeeper, Con Sullivan. The whistle blew, and Evans, perhaps a frustrated goal scorer that day, took a powerful shot from almost 40 yards that was nailed under crossbar of his own goal. Sullivan dove to repel the ball but could do nothing to avoid the visitor's team pulling one back. Pulling one back? Yes. It happened that the whistle heard by Evans did not come from the referee, but from a comedian sitting on the stands. The referee validated the goal and, a second later, blew his whistle again to end the game. Evans was able to remove the bad taste the following year, when he was designated to shoot the penalty kicks. Thus, he scored 12 goals (in favor), in 189 presentations with the Gunners' shirt.

19 RED CARDS IN THE COPA LIBERTADORES

Group 1 of the initial round of the 1971 Copa Libertadores was very even. After seven matches, all the teams—the Argentineans Boca Juniors and Rosario Central, and the Peruvians Universitario de Deportes and Sporting Cristal—had won, lost, and tied, leaving an open end for the last five clashes, four of them scheduled in Argentine territory, in pursuit of the only place available for the semifinals. On Wednesday, March 17, 1971, Boca received Sporting Cristal with some reluctance, considering that the Peruvians had played with lots of energy and made strong tackles at the first meeting at the National Stadium in Lima. In a packed "Bombonera," Juan Orbegoso from the Peruvian squad opened the scoring at 17 minutes, but Boca was able to turn it around quickly at 22 and 24 minutes with goals from Jorge Coch and Angel Clemente Rojas, the latter after stopping a cross from the right with his chest and shooting inside the penalty box, scoring against visiting goalkeeper Luis Rubiños. The partial victory was leaving Boca well positioned to take over the top place in the standings. But Sporting did not give up and balanced the score at 69 minutes with a goal by Carlos Gonzáles Pajuelo, who sent a ball that had escaped from the hands of the Boca goalkeeper Rubén Sánchez—he was trying to collect a strike from a distance from Alberto Gallardo—to the back of the empty goal. The draw fired up the emotions of the host soccer players, desperate for the key victory that escaped them. One minute from the end, Boca's impotence ignited the fuse of the most devastating bomb in the history of the Copa Libertadores. Vessilio Bártoli, the Argentinean coach of the Peruvian team, recalled in a television interview that the scandal broke out when Boca defender Roberto Rogel, turned into a striker, "grabbed (Fernando) Mellán from the neck and threw him to the ground. (Uruguayan ref) Alejandro Otero called 'foul' in favor of Cristal, but Rogel called for a 'penalty.'" According to the chronicles of the time, the situation, which did not go beyond struggles and threats, exploded when the Argentine Rubén Suñé knocked down Gallardo. From there, soccer playing gave way to a flurry of punches and kicks that seemed more like the struggles at the legendary Roman Colosseum. One of the leading gladiators was Suñé, who chased Gallardo with a flag from the corner that had been torn from its original site. The Peruvian striker, instead of escaping, waited for Boca's defender and kicked him in the face, breaking his cheekbone. In another part of the field, Eloy Campos from the away team was thrown to the ground and, while there, was kicked violently, fracturing his nasal septum. When, several minutes later, the police managed to break up the fighting, the referee Otero took out his red card to showed it 19 times and ended the game. Only the goalkeepers Sánchez and Rubiños and the host defender Julio Meléndez from Peru were saved from being sent off. After the players went through the showers, all those who had been red-carded were taken to a police station in compliance with the Edict of Sports Meetings.

Well, not all, because Eloy Campos and Fernando Mellán had to be hospitalized for the tremendous beating they received. The 17 prisoners occupied the same cell and regained their freedom the following afternoon, thanks to the tireless efforts of consuls and ambassadors of both countries, and an extensive telephone call between the two presidents of Argentina and Peru, Juan Carlos

Onganía and Juan Velasco Alvarado, who, coincidentally, were both military men and had led a coup d'etat to the constitutional governments of Arturo Illia and Fernando Belaúnde Terry, respectively. Alfredo Quesada said that the morning after the huge fight, Meléndez showed up at the police headquarters with "coffee and cookies for everyone." At the end, "we made friends at the police station, because nobody wanted to be in that situation."

When studying the case, CONMEBOL awarded Sporting Cristal the two points and Boca the loss. The leaders of the Buenos Aires team considered the decision unfair and decided not to show up to play the two remaining games against Universitario in Buenos Aires and against Rosario Central in Arroyito. In this way, the great beneficiary was Universitario, which remained in first place in the group and went to the semifinal of the tournament.

ONE FOR TWO

While meticulously researching the stories included in this book, I stumbled across a slightly bizarre occurrence: a goal awarded to two players. The official record of the Football Association of England awarded a goal from the London club Chelsea FC, jointly, half and half, or, to put it more appropriately, "fifty-fifty," to Jack Froggatt and Stan Milburn. The amazing and exceptional goal took place on December 18, 1954, at the Stamford Bridge stadium in the British capital and was settled by referee Arthur Ellis. This odd situation has an even stranger side note, as it is necessary to point out that Froggatt and Milburn did not wear the Chelsea jersey, but rather the Leicester City FC jersey, the rival of the London club that afternoon in the first division league. With a blank scoreboard, the two defenders rushed to clear a rival cross with voracious readiness, determined lack of skill, and, of course, bad luck. The couple reached the ball at the same moment, putting together a ridiculous standing sandwich that sent the ball right toward the net of the goal defended by their surprised Scottish teammate, John Anderson. Chelsea won that day by 3 to 1, but the bronze was left for the opening of the scoreboard: The only goal in the history scored by two different players and, above all, an own goal!

AS IF WITH THE HAND

After 16 years, the St. Andrews Stadium was once again the scene of the Birmingham City derby between Birmingham City FC and Aston Villa FC, one of the fiercest duels in England. On September 16, 2002, the home squad, who had wandered through the second and even the third division before returning to the first and had suffered the acid jokes of their Aston Villa rivals for a decade and a half, opened the scoring at the 31st minute thanks to a shot by Clinton Morrison. But the Blues' sweet revenge would come in the second half at minute 77. Aston Villa's right-back, the Swedish Olof Mellberg, made a sideline throw in to his goalkeeper, Peter Enckelman from Finland. The goalkeeper, perhaps confident, perhaps nervous because the draw didn't come fast enough, tried to stop the ball with his left foot, but the ball slipped under his sole and ended up inside the goal. After the match, Enckelman said he hadn't touched the ball—the television playbacks seem to agree with him—so the referee David Elleray should have canceled the goal and called for a corner kick for the host team. As the regulation states: If the ball enters the goal of the team performing the throw-in directly from the throw-in, the referee must award a corner kick. "I tried to control the ball, but it went under my foot without me touching it," explained Enckelman, who admitted that this was "the worst moment" of his career. The bizarre situation was celebrated by a fan of Birmingham City, who jumped on the field to mock the unhappy goalkeeper with rude gestures and even a sarcastic slap. Aston

Villa lost 3-0 that day, but for Enckelman, at least, there was a small consolation: The fan who had mocked him, Michael Harper, was sentenced by a Birmingham judge to four months in prison and six years without being able to assist a soccer game. At least it's something.

WIN WITHOUT SCORING?

Own goals generate two opposite moods: disappointment and anger in the disadvantaged team, enthusiasm and laughter for the squad that receives such an unexpected gift. In fact, there have been cases of teams that have won a match without performing a single kick or header into the opponent's goal. One of the most famous of recent times occurred in the victory of Granada CF over Real Madrid CF, part of the first division in Spain, in February 2013. The Andalusian squad won 1-0 without a single shot to their opponents' goal, and with their only one goal being an own goal by none other than the great star and top scorer of the institution from the capital: the Portuguese Cristiano Ronaldo.

UNUSUAL EJECTIONS

According to the regulations approved by the FIFA International Board, there are seven circumstances under which a player may be expelled from the game: Being guilty of serious rough play; being guilty of violent conduct; spitting at an opponent or any other person; intentionally preventing a goal or an obvious goal opportunity with the hand (this does not apply to the goalkeeper in his own penalty area); denying an obvious goal-scoring opportunity to an opponent moving toward the player's goal by an offence punishable by a free kick or a penalty kick; using offensive, rude, or obscene language or gestures of the same nature; and receiving a second warning in the same match. Which of these points did the Bolivian referee Ignacio Salvatierra cite in order to directly expel striker Abel Vaca Saucedo? In October of 1996, Vaca Saucedo from the Germán Pommier team from the Amazonian city of Trinidad made a fantastic goal that included several dribbles and a masterful Rabona ending. When the skilled attacker finished celebrating, Salvatierra approached him and, instead of congratulating him, showed him the red card. According to the referee, the skillful Vaca Saucedo "had humiliated" his rivals with such a spectacular goal. In short, he red-carded him for being too "skillful." When the poor kid asked for an explanation, the man in black responded in anger; not only did he rebuke him harshly for his treatment of the members of the rival team, Jaille, but he also asked him to take "the practice of the sport more seriously."

Another player who still doesn't understand why he was expelled is the Czech David Zoubek. On May 7, 2000, referee Karel Krula showed him the red card...because his back number had fallen off! The problem started when FC Hradec Králové's Zoubek replaced a teammate in a match against Prague's Bohemians for the Czech first division. As soon as he stepped onto the grass, Krula told the forward that one of the ones of his "11" had come off. The attacker returned to the bench, and his trainer attempted to fix the problem with a piece of tape. But, after a few minutes, the number was back on the ground, so Krula, undoubtedly a man of little patience, took out his red card and threw out the surprised Zoubek, who surely remembered to curse all the relatives of the referee and the club's props.

RETURN FROM HELL

What else can be said about Stoke City FC England striker Jonathan "Jon" Walters? On Saturday, January 12, 2013, Walters lived a nightmare against Chelsea FC: In just 90 minutes, he scored two own goals and missed a penalty shot! With such (involuntary) help, the London team had no problem prevailing 0-4. But soccer, affirms one of the grandstand axioms, sooner or later grants you revenge, and the infamous goal scorer had it. Three days later, during the fourth round of the FA Cup, Stoke defeated Crystal Palace FC 4 to 1. The first 90 minutes of this match—which, like the duel with Chelsea, were played at the Britannia Stadium—had finished 1-1. In extra time, Walters scored two goals that sealed the home win and dispelled the dark clouds of the weekend.

CHICKENS

On May 20, 1966, at the National Stadium in Santiago de Chile, the Argentine club River Plate was defeating Uruguayan Peñarol 2-0 in the tiebreaker game of the Copa Libertadores final. River was not only defeating their rival on the scoreboard: the black-and-gold soccer players were lost inside the field, and they could do little to contain the constant attacks of their opponents from River Plate. However, halfway through the second half, the attitude of the Uruguayans changed radically after the Argentinian goalkeeper Amadeo Carrizo stopped a header from the Peruvian striker Juan Joya. "That was not liked by the players of Peñarol," said the journalist who announced the game live for Argentina. Indeed, after River Plate's goalkeeper's bluff, Peñarol equalized the score with a goal from Ecuador's Alberto Spencer and another from Julio César Abbadie, although this second goal could be awarded an own goal by the Uruguayan "millionaire" Roberto Matosas, who diverted the Abbadie shot and dislodged Carrizo. In extra time, the Uruguayan team knocked out their opponents with a second goal by Spencer and one by Pedro Rocha. Peñarol lifted the continental trophy and made the Olympic lap while the River players left the pitch crestfallen, lamenting the lost opportunity to be champions of South America. One of the men, Ermindo Onega, remarked years later that "it was incredible" how the title escaped them. "When they scored the third goal, Abbadie told me: 'Only you guys lose a match like that.'" Onega lamented that, apart from being out of the historical bronze, they squandered "a month's vacation on the French Riviera, which (the then president from River, Antonio) Liberti had promised us if we won." The "millionaire" coach, Renato Cesarini, affirmed that "they betrayed me" and, although he never revealed the names of those who, according to his suspicions, had "sold out," he seemed to imply it was the two Uruguayans from his squad, Matosas and Luis Cubilla. Cesarini—who took his suspicions to the grave—was also questioned for having replaced right-back Alberto Sainz, who had been injured, by forward Juan Carlos Lallana, a fact that forced a tactical restructuring of the entire team. Meanwhile, Néstor "Tito" Gonçalves, a brave Peñarol midfielder, proclaimed in an interview with the Argentine magazine *El Gráfico* that "the change was produced by us at the beginning of the second half. We thought that, more than tactical changes, what we needed was to change the game's climate to stave off the embarrassment; we became desperate and resorted to illicit plays. That's true, we talked to them and we even told them that, if they won, we would go to look for them in the dressing room and at the hotel. Things happened in such a way that it was a climate of war from which we got a great advantage before the passivity of River. I noticed the temperamental difference the next day. In the airport cafeteria when the two teams met, one of us went to speak over the loudspeakers and asked: 'Who is River's dad?' And another voice answered: 'Peñarol!' That was heard throughout the airport and the laughter overwhelmed all present. We wanted to die; we lowered our heads in shame. If that happened the other way around, we would have pummeled them. We would not accept such a joke that they accepted without fuss."

River returned to their country and a week later faced Club Atlético Banfield away for the first division tournament in Argentina. During the second half of that game, the local fans launched a white chicken with a red stripe painted on its plumage into the penalty box that was guarded by the Carrizo's replacement, Hugo Gatti. The act was supposed to show the cowardice displayed by River players against Peñarol. The bird, visibly scared, ran across the pitch and crossed the entire field. The mischief not only caused the Banfield fans to laugh, but it was highlighted by all the newspapers the following day. The new nickname, which emerged on May 29, 1966, lasts until today. But, half a century after that episode, the derisive nickname has been reinvented. At present, it is the River Plate sympathizers themselves who identify themselves with the feathers. Every soccer day, at the Monumental stadium, you can hear how the red-and-white fans announce that they are going to the stadium "to cheer for the chickens."

THE PATRON OF EVIL

In 2011, the TV program *Pura Química* (*Pure Chemistry*) of the *ESPN* network in Argentina had the former international referee Juan Bava as a guest on the show. During the interview, the former referee recalled a dramatic episode he had to suffer when, along with two other colleagues, he had to referee the second leg of the semifinal of the 1989 Copa Libertadores between Atlético Nacional de Colombia and Danubio Fútbol Club of Uruguay in the city of Medellín. The night before this match—the first leg match had ended without goals in Montevideo—a local referee, Octavio Sierra, took his foreign colleagues to dinner. During the meal, Sierra reported several episodes of violence suffered by refs of the Colombian league and shockingly then took them in his car to a place where they had killed one of the men, allegedly by order of drug trafficker Pablo Escobar. The Argentines returned to the hotel feeling very frightened, but the terror did not end with Sierra's stories. "We went to bed, and at dawn they broke the door, split it straight through the middle, and three or four people entered with machine guns and started jumping over the beds. I was curled up in a corner. I indicated, pointing to Carlos Esposito the referee, 'talk to him.' One, the boss, says 'here is the money. Nacional has to win.' They left a box in which, they said, there was a 'green stick' (a million dollars, which Bava, in the report, claimed that none of the Argentines touched) and left. It was six in the morning, and Esposito smoked and smoked. I said, 'Carlitos, this is outrageous. So it's very clear: If these guys don't win, I'll go into the field with five minutes left and I myself will head it into the top corner of the goal. Do you understand? We're going to make them win, Carlitos. I have two children to raise, they can't kill me here." When asked how that match had ended, Bava replied, bluntly: "Six to zero, Nacional victory." Atlético Nacional went on to the final, which, after each home team won 2-0 in both legs, they won due to the penalty against Olimpia of Paraguay and became champion of the Libertadores.

CARELESS HANDS

Leeds United AFC Welsh goalkeeper Gary Sprake picked up the cross sent from the corner spot and tried to quickly throw the ball with his right hand toward his teammate Terry Cooper to start an effective counterattack. But, when he had started the movement to pass the ball, the goalkeeper noticed that Cooper was guarded by the left back of Liverpool FC, Ian Callaghan. Sprake tried, desperately, to stop the throw, but his effort was useless: when folding his arm, the ball escaped from his hand, backwards, and ended...inside his goal! An unusual goal that made the 40,000 red fans who filled Anfield Road on that December afternoon in 1967 laugh. That goal, scored at 44 minutes, closed the first half with a 2-0 for the home squad. At halftime, while the coach Don Revie and the rest of the Leeds players tried to calm down the dejected Sprake, the cruel DJ of the stadium played, from his turntable, the song "Careless Hands" by Des O'Connor. Since then, every time the Welshman came on the field—the next six seasons with Leeds and two with Birmingham City FC—the rival fan bases received him by singing "Carless Hands."

THE AGREEMENT

On the night of April 5, 1991, the stadium Camilo Cichero (former name of La Bombonera of Argentine club Boca Juniors) was the scene of a parody that was more theater than soccer. That day, the *xeneize* team faced the Oriente Petrolero Sports Club of Bolivia. A draw would qualify the two clubs along with Bolívar, first place of the four, to the detriment of River Plate, last of group 1, who had played all their matches in the initial round of the Copa Libertadores of that year. In that time, the best three of each group passed to the next phase. After Uruguayan referee Ernesto Filippi whistled the start of the match, the 22 players passed the ball from one side to the other, without reaching any of the boxes, in an obvious agreement that made all the players and also the Boca fans very happy. The home fans celebrated with an "olé" or applause each ball passed by the rival defenders to their goalkeeper, Darío Rojas. The only one who dared to disobey the unusual pact was Diego Latorre, who came in as a substitute at 15 minutes of the second half. As soon as he captured the ball, he approached the Bolivian box and took a shot that disturbed Rojas, but didn't reach the goal. The audacity of the current sports journalist was punished by a massive whistle from all sides of the stadium. The last minutes of the "duel" were nothingness itself. The radio announcer Víctor Hugo Morales, outraged, left the transmission of the match due to the evident lack of real play. When Filippi ended the farce, the Boca fans celebrated the elimination of their classic opponent as if the team had won the Club World Cup. Interviewed on the *Gente de Fútbol* program of the Bolivian channel *Activa TV*, striker Francisco Takeo, who was sitting on the substitute bench that day, revealed that "El Abuelo" (the Old Man)—who was then Boca's hooligans' boss—entered their locker room before the game and said: "Little Bolivians, everything is already talked about with the Boca players. The match has to finish tied to keep the 'chickens' out of the Cup. Do not get distracted because if you do, you don't come out alive from here." The referee Filippi, irritated by what he had had to endure, presented a report to CONMEBOL for the "lack of effort" of the players. The paper must remain archived among other misplaced reports.

WHY DID YOU EVEN COME?

In 1884, the Football Association Amateur Cup was put into play for the first time, a contest that didn't allow professional clubs or soccer players to participate and that summoned, in general, teams of secondary schools or universities. The first final was contested between Old Carthusians Football Club—a team made up of students from the Charterhouse School of Surrey County—and Casuals Football Club, which was mostly made up of boys from two London schools: Eton and Westminster. Old Carthusians reached the climactic match after defeating Bishop Auckland 5-1 in the semifinals, while Casuals had beaten Sherwood Foresters 1-0.

On April 7, at the Richmond Athletic Ground, the two teams showed up to start the clash, but one of them, Casuals, had only ten men; the one missing, Lewis Vaughan Lodge, had missed his train from English capital, a distance of about 6 miles. The referee was kind enough to wait 20 minutes, but as Lodge didn't appear and the 3,500 spectators were getting impatient, he ordered the start of the match. Despite the disadvantage, it was Casuals who opened the scoring, through their fullback, Charles Hatton, at 9 minutes. Shortly after, Lodge appeared, changed, and entered the field to complete his team, which continued to lead the match. Maybe because he was cold, possibly upset by his lateness, the first ball that Lodge touched ended up inside the

159

goal...of Casuals. Old Carthusians finally won 2-1 and became the first champion of the FA Amateur Cup. The companions of Lodge, meanwhile, showered, changed, and cooled their heads before asking the delayed soccer player "why the hell didn't you stay at home?"

ECSTASY

"The extravagant acts of joy should not be sentenced as corruption of our sport. Is it not just the joy of the goal, the overwhelming joy of victory, the exuberant emotion (which, most of us in our time are only able to express in the stadiums) that contribute most to the global success of football? The joy of the scorer is one of the most natural aspects of the sport, a repetitive culmination for each soccer player, an emotional climax that can only be enjoyed if he can share his joy with the spectators. Positive emotions such as this spontaneous joy should not be tarnished with an act of punishment. Punishing enthusiasm with yellow cards does not correspond to the spirit of our game. Goals must be celebrated as they come. We continue to rejoice freely for joy in the goals and for the pleasure in soccer." Surely, if you tried to guess who said this, you won't guess the correct name even if you have dozens of guesses. These concepts correspond to the president of FIFA, Joseph Blatter, and were published in the *FIFA Magazine* of December 1984, when the Swiss occupied the general secretariat of the governing body of soccer. Years later, these statements are a curiosity in themselves, because it is FIFA that has set limits to those same "extravagant acts" pondered by Blatter. Rule 12 of the soccer code, referring to "faults and inaccuracies," warns that "even though a player is allowed to express his happiness when he scores a goal, the celebration should not be excessive. Reasonable celebrations are allowed.

The practice of choreographed celebrations should be discouraged if they cause an excessive loss of time. In this case, the referees must intervene. A player must be warned if, in the opinion of the referee, he makes provocative, ridiculous, or extravagant gestures; climbs to the peripheral fences to celebrate a goal; takes off his shirt over his head, or covers his head with his shirt; and covers the head or face with a mask or similar items." It is clarified that "the act of leaving the field to celebrate a goal is not in itself a punishable offense with warning, but it is essential that players return to the field of play as soon as possible. It is intended that referees act in a preventive manner and use common sense when facing goal celebrations." These rules are generally followed, but there is always some vivacious chap who, overwhelmed by ecstasy, unleashes his frenzy without thinking about the consequences.

Genoa CFC, the blue-and-red Ligurian team, was fighting for promotion to the Italian Serie A at home against Atalanta de Bergamo, one of the leaders of the Second Division championship, so it was necessary to win. No other result was possible that afternoon of April 28, 2000. The clash, full of friction, nerves, and a strong leg, was evenly matched, until the speedy and blond forward Davide Nicola executed a withering cross that overcame the dive of visiting goalkeeper Alberto Fontana. While the Luigi Ferraris stadium exploded with joy, the striker extended his crazy run to the side of the field, where a group of policemen (and policewomen) were sitting, and threw himself at a beautiful law enforcement officer, whom he kissed fervently on the mouth. It was—the coveted soccer player later acknowledged—a "friend" who had "fallen into his net" of skillful nymph fisherman. Nicola was not punished for such a passionate celebration, but the one who saw the red card was the woman: Her husband, who was watching the game live on television, immediately called her cell phone and expelled her from the marital bed. Apparently, the husband had not heard of Blatter's recommendations.

THE FORCE OF NATURE

The Colombian club Once Caldas is known as "the whites" because of its traditional uniform. For that reason, it was fortunate for Jhon Viáfara that, for the first final of the 2004 Copa Libertadores against Boca Juniors played at La Bombonera in Buenos Aires on June 23, the squad from Manizales would have chosen an alternative uniform. As soon as the whistle that started the game blew, Viáfara began to feel an intestinal discomfort that, as time went on, became intolerable. "It must be the energy drinks," thought the midfielder, who asked Uruguayan referee Gustavo Méndez to stop the game and allow him to decompress his ailment in the locker room. But the judge refused: that license is only contemplated for the goalie. Viáfara did not want to leave his team for several minutes with a man down during the most important match in their history. Therefore, at 30 minutes, he decided to relieve his stomach pain...standing and in middle of the vital match! It was fortunate for Jhon Viáfara that Once Caldas came out on the field with a completely black uniform that night. Neither the implacable eye of the television nor the fans noticed any abnormality in the midfielder. Those who did notice that something infrequent had happened were the home players, who must have held their breath each time they had to mark the aromatic rival. At halftime, the Colombian was able to change his uniform, and the match ended without goals. Eight days later, Viáfara opened the score in the rematch, which ended 1 to 1 and allowed the Manizales club to get their first continental title through a penalty shootout. That glorious day, Once Caldas did wear his characteristic white uniform, but the scorer didn't care. His problem had been left behind.

AN EPIDEMIC

CA Platense had been unstoppable. The "brown" team had given CA Estudiantes a tremendous thrashing in their field of La Plata during the first half of the match played on May 10, 1942, for the first division tournament in Argentina. The visiting club had gone to halftime with an unquestionable 0-3 in favor that had frightened many of the fans of the "Lion" directly out of the stadium. During the break, the visiting players cheered their remarkable performance by drinking *mate cocido* (a type of tea), a very popular infusion in Argentina. Only this time, instead of the traditional *yerba* (tea leaves), which could not be obtained, one of Brazilian origin was used to prepare the drink. When returning to the lawn, the boys from Platense felt an immediate intestinal breakdown that destroyed their resistance. With the exception of José Roberto Toledo, who had refrained from drinking *mate*, ten men could scarcely stand upright. Without the possibility of making substitutions, not yet allowed by the rules, the good game Platense had played was weakened, and Estudiantes won by a surprising 7 to 3. Although the final whistle sounded at 5 PM, the bus with the defeated players could only leave at 8 PM, and unfortunately the toilets in the locker room had proven insufficient. The almost 40 miles from La Plata to the city of Buenos Aires were endless. The bus had to make several stops at bars bordering the road. Cooked *mate* was not prepared again for the "squid," as Platense players and fans are known.

On October 11, 1992, the Ethiopian national team arrived in the city of Casablanca with great hopes of obtaining a good result against Morocco in the opening match of the African qualifiers for the 1994 World Cup. But, with the passing of time, the visiting squad began to lose players affected by a brutal diarrhea that was most likely caused by a not-so-fresh lunch. The coach was forced to make the two subs allowed after only a few minutes, but the epidemic continued, and the "waliya boyz" dropped like flies. The game was suspended at 55 minutes with the score 5-0 and only six Ethiopians on the field. The rest of the boys fought each other to occupy the "thrones" of the locker room.

Another food complication—in this case, rotten fish—decimated Stoke City FC when they faced Liverpool FC at Anfield Road stadium on January 4, 1902, in a first division game. Stoke finished the game with only seven players on the field and a 7-0 adverse result on the scoreboard. The great beneficiary of the afternoon was Andy McGuigan, who took advantage of the misfortune of others to become the first Liverpool player to score five goals in a single match.

CA Ciclón, from the Bolivian city of Tarija, failed to appear at the Yoyo Zambrano stadium to face Atlético Pompeya in Trinidad for the semifinal of the 1999 Copa Simón Bolívar that would promote a team to the first division. All Cyclone soccer players had been disturbed by acute general diarrhea. In this case, the leaders of Ciclón denounced to the press that they suspected a maneuver perpetrated by "people linked" to the rival institution. Atlético Pompeya went through the round and then went up a division by beating Mariscal Braun.

UNSOLICITED AID

The intention of referee Thomas Essbach, of the now defunct German Democratic Republic, wasn't bad. The situation of the player Carsten Saenger—capped 18 times for the former socialist state—made him feel pity. Saenger had been in the bathroom for almost an hour and could not comply with anti-doping control because he was unable to pee. Saenger drank lots of water, but the dehydration suffered during the match by the local league didn't lessen. "Let's see, kid. I'll help you," Essbach said helpingly as he filled the jar for the "dry" soccer player while those responsible for the test looked the other way. The real problem happened a few days later, when the urine sample showed "positive." The referee had forgotten that he had been treated against a cold with a drug that contained substances that were on the list of products banned by FIFA. Saenger and Essbach finally admitted the mischief, and both were punished. Popular knowledge affirms that, sometimes, "the remedy is worse than the disease."

THE DRAW

On May 7, 1961, at the Nemesio Camacho stadium El Campin in Bogotá, a solitary goal against visiting goalkeeper Óscar Claure Méndez resulted in a draw between the Club Independiente Santa Fe of Colombia and Club Deportivo Jorge Wilstermann of Bolivia at the quarterfinals of the Copa Libertadores. After a 3-2 at the Félix Capriles stadium of Cochabamba and the narrow 1 to 0 in the Colombian capital, the duel was equaled in points and goal difference (back then, it wasn't taken into account if they were scored at a home or away game). Since at that time the incorporation of the series of shots from the penalty spot to resolve a situation such as this had not been made official, the regulation discussed if the contest should be resolved with a third match. At first, the directors of the two teams agreed to play that match in El Campín the following Sunday, May 14. But, according to the newspaper *El Tiempo* of Bogotá in its Tuesday edition on May 9, 1961, the representatives of the Bolivian team reversed the agreement because with the one-week stay in the coffee capital "they would lose 10,000 dollars." To resolve the dispute, the leaders of both squads agreed to hold a draw at the headquarters of the ADEFUTBOL (denomination that the Colombian Football Federation was part of at that time), to unlock the parity without the need to play. "Two ballots were arranged to decide the team that would continue in the Campeonato de Campeones de America, the one from Wilstermann, signed by Jorge Rojas, and the one from Santa Fe, by Jorge Ferro. Jorge

Garcés, a former member of the ADEFUTBOL, was assigned to pick the winning ballot. The first one that was taken out indicated the team that would be eliminated. When the ballot was taken out, it was Eduardo de Castro's turn to read the name of Jorge Wilstermann to announce their elimination. So, three Jorges took part in the elimination of a fourth Jorge, Wilstermann." *El Tiempo* reported. The delegation accepted the result and returned to Cochabamba; however, a couple of decades later, Jorge Rojas Tardío, who had been president of Wilstermann when that key match was played, denounced that the draw was a fraud. "After many years we learned that CONMEBOL's decision was to eliminate Wilstermann and qualify Santa Fe to the semifinals." Rojas Tardío said, adding that "the two pieces of paper that were in the hat on the day of the draw had the name of Wilstermann" and that "the referee of that match (the Argentine Luis Ventre) confessed to us that he had been forced to proceed in that way" and to support the alleged fraud. The truth was that, with or without tricks, the Cardinals went on to the semifinals where they were eliminated by the Sociedade Esportiva Palmeiras of Brazil after a 2-2 draw in Bogotá and an unquestionable 4 to 1 in the municipal stadium Paulo Machado de Carvalho of San Pablo, also known as "Pacaembú."

KEEPING COUNT

The Brazilian referee Francisco Lima started counting: one, two, three, four, five, six...the amount did not make sense. He had drawn four red cards, but the Naútico club, which on April 15, 2003, had started the match with eleven against Rio Negro, only had six players. Where was the seventh? Rio Negro was winning 5-0 when, at 72 minutes, Lima sent out his fourth player from Naútico. Seconds before resuming play in the Flamarion Vasconcelos stadium, the referee felt that something was not right and decided to check how many men were left in the black-and-red striped shirt, identical to that of the Italian team Associazione Calcio Milan. That's when he noticed that a player had disappeared without him or his assistants realizing it. Lima called the Naútico captain over, and, since the captain didn't know where his teammate was, Lima ended the match. "It was his only successful call of the day," muttered one of the players from the thrashed team.

THE BIG ESCAPE

It could be said that the performance of the Italian team Rimini Calcio FC was heroic. With three fewer players, all red-carded, they managed a valuable 1-1 at home, the Romeo Neri stadium, against Castel San Pietro Terme Calcio for the Lega Pro Seconda Divisione of the Serie C. However, despite the epic feat that these men achieved that April 26, 1998, the mood of the "tifosi" was simmering with rage. They blamed the referee Antonio Manari for having taken away, with his unfair red cards, what, before the match, seemed an indisputable triumph against a weak rival. With the final whistle, the fans jumped on the field and ran to Manari, hoping to teach him a lesson or two about making the right calls. The referee took refuge in his locker room just before the fans could catch him and skin him alive. The police intervened and cleared the field and the area of the locker room, but hundreds of rabid people remained outside the stadium, uttering threats and throwing stones and other projectiles. As there was no possible or safe exit by land, the local police requested assistance from the *Guardia di Finanza*, a special security corps dependent on the Ministries of Economy and the Interior. This group sent a special force and arranged for a helicopter to land on the field to evacuate the referee and his assistants. Manari was thus able to return safely to Teramo, his city. He never came back to Rimini.

THE UNLUCKY HUG

In January of 1989, the Venezuelan champion Club Sport Marítimo was tying 1-1 at home with Arroceros de Calabozo FC, at that time the most modest team in the first division of the South American nation. Just when the match seemed destined to end in a draw, the Brazilian striker Edilberto got the goal that gave Marítimo the victory. The goal unleashed Edilberto's euphoria, and, happy with his aim, he embraced the first player that crossed his crazy run. And the first one was, unfortuantely, the referee Antonio López. When he recovered from the unexpected show of affection, the referee extracted his red card and threw out the affectionate scorer. A very insensitive referee, indeed.

EXHIBITIONISTS

In some cases, warnings and ejections fall short, and, rather than sending them to the showers, the effusive celebrators would be better off getting an appointment with the psychologist. In December of 1995, in the Paraguayan department of Guairá, Villarrica's center forward, Carlos Román, couldn't seem to come up with a better way to celebrate his goal than to drop his pants to his knees. "I do not know what happened to me. I eluded the goalkeeper, I went into the goal with the ball on my feet, and I got excited," the exuberant attacker tried to explain. He was immediately red-carded. In spite of continuing with ten men most of the match—Román was thrown out at the 38th minute of the first half—the team from Villarrica bested the representative of San José by 3 to 0.

More upsetting than the defeat, the fans of FC Mragovia, a team of a Polish regional league, were horrified when the scorer of LKS Reduta Bisztynek, Zbigniew Romanowski, displayed his penis after each goal. The day after the game—which was played in April 1998—the offended fans sent a protest letter to the newspaper *Gazeta Olsztynska* because they could no longer tolerate Romanowski's rudeness and the complacency of the referee, who did not punish the surly forward.

In April 2000, an Iranian soccer player was suspended for life by a court in that Islamic country for lowering his pants and taking an

Olympic lap in his underpants while celebrating his goal. Mohsen Rassuli, a young attacker for the Saypa FC club in Tehran, scored in the 119th minute the goal that meant victory for his team in the semifinals of the Iran Cup against PAS FC, their traditional rival. The exaggerated display of celebration was not only seen by the crowd that filled the stadium, but the match was also broadcast live on state television, which usually cuts these types of scenes in international matches. The case of Rassuli was considered so grave that it was transferred directly to the national justice before being evaluated by the Disciplinary Committee of the Iranian Soccer Federation. To the harsh penalty was added a fine equivalent to $33,000, which the athlete paid half in cash and half in installments.

Many goal scorers often remove their shirts and flip them over their heads to celebrate an important goal, although the overflow of happiness costs them a yellow. In April 2001, the Brazilian William of the club Ponta Porã Sociedade Esportiva of Mato Grosso joined in doing the "helicopter" after opening the score against Nova Andradina FC, but he decorated the popular celebration with an original touch: Instead of using his t-shirt as "blades," he used his pants. William was thrown out at once, his decimated team finally lost, and, to make matters worse, the police arrested the daring scorer prisoner for obscene display and public nuisance. However, since every cloud has a silver lining, among such adversity a fresh air of revenge arose when the euphoric William was hired to participate in...an underwear publicity campaign!

EXPELLED BY HIS CAPTAIN

On October 18, 1914, forward Francisco Fuentes made his debut as a starter in the Boca Juniors first team, until then a regular subscriber to watching the matches from the stands. At that time, subs were not allowed, and the benches had not been incorporated. Boca received Comercio that afternoon at their stadium in the town of Wilde (predecessor of the famous Bombonera). Fuentes, eager to win a place among the starters at any price, decided to apply all kinds of aggressive stratagems to overcome his rivals. More than playing soccer, the stout attacker dedicated himself to lashing out violently against his opponents, whether or not they had the ball in their possession, and to hit them with his fists and elbows when the match referee turned his back on him. But, contrary to what Fuentes expected, his methodology caused an unpleasant impression on the Boca fans, to such an extent that the player came out of the game to fight with the spectators who disapproved of his attitude. Fortunately, several members of the local board of directors intervened in time to force the debutant to desist and return to the match. His team was so embarrassed that Donato Abbatángelo, their captain, decided to take it upon himself to expel the bellicose Fuente from the grounds. The blue-and-gold squad continued the action with ten men, a fact that did not prevent them from triumphing, finally, by 1 to 0, thanks to the goal scored by Francisco Taggino at the 73rd minute.

LUCKY SHOES

The soccer cleats brought especially from Italy were perfect on the feet of Liverpool striker Michael Owen. The young star of the English team was delighted with his new, comfortable, and fluffy shoes, which the sports shoe company that hired him as a model had given him to wear in the final of the 2001 FA Cup against Arsenal. However, when the Liverpool coach, Frenchman Gerard Houllier, saw Owen with his brand-new footwear inside the locker room at Cardiff's Millennium Stadium, he ordered him to take them off immediately and put on his old boots. "Use the old ones," Houiller demanded. "They are the ones that have helped you score all your goals." The striker, who had scored six goals in the previous three games, thought the coach was joking. However, Houiller was adamant: If Michael didn't obey, he would wear his new shoes sitting on the bench. Michael finally gave in and put on his old and worn booties. Fate proved the Frenchman right: Liverpool defeated Arsenal that day by 2 to 1, with two goals from Owen. When returning to the locker room, with his champion medal hanging from his neck, the scorer embraced with the coach, who congratulated him for his performance, but even more for having obeyed the order to use the magical "lucky shoes." The ones not happy at all were the higher-ups at the sports shoe company. They didn't know what to do with the thousand pairs of shoes that they planned to launch on the market the day after the glittering final.

GOD'S FORWARD

When the three-time champions of the Copa Libertadores went out onto the turf of their traditional Jorge Luis Hirschi stadium, located in the city of La Plata, neither the players nor the fans felt, even slightly, that the undefeated streak Estudiantes held in that coliseum in the South American tournament could end that day, April 29, 1971, when they played against the allegedly weak Barcelona Sporting Club of Ecuador. The reasons for them were plenty: On that field, now demolished, Estudiantes had strung together eleven games without a loss against very hard squads such as the Argentines River, Racing and Independiente, the Uruguayans Peñarol and Nacional, and the Brazilian Palmeiras. In addition, because the team had beaten Barcelona in Guayaquil 1 to 0 with a goal by Juan Echecopar a few days before, confidence was high. However, miracles do occur often in soccer. In this case, one could say that literally, because Barcelona prevailed by one goal thanks by Juan Manuel Bazurko, a Basque who, besides being a soccer player, was also a priest!

Bazurko—born in Mutriku in 1944 and former CD Motrico player—was ordained as a Catholic priest in the late 60s, and in 1969 he was sent to the parish of San Camilo de Quevedo, in the province of Los Rios of Ecuador. There, while taking care of the church of San Cristóbal, Bazurko indulged in his passion for soccer. On Saturdays, the priest stood out as a fast and powerful striker, owner of a lethal header, in the regional championships.

First, in 1969, he broke the nets for the San Camilo Sports Club; then, in 1970, he wore the jersey of Liga Deportiva Universitaria de Portoviejo. His effectiveness aroused the interest of Barcelona, who had qualified for the Libertadores of 1971 as national champion of the previous season. Authorized by the bishopric, the unusual forward, who had promised to donate his salary as a player to the parish of San Camilo, moved his goals to Guayaquil. Although his coach, the Brazilian Otto Viera, did not really appreciate him, he put him as a starter against the three-time champion Estudiantes. Perhaps by divine design, the priest was the author of the only goal of the game at 63 minutes.

The career of the priest Bazurko did not last much longer. After the elimination in the semifinals of the Libertadores, despite the resounding victory against the continental monarch, and having won the first division Ecuadorian championship, the priest hung up his cleats and changed the shirt and shorts for the cassock, although not permanently. A few years later, he returned to the Basque Country, left the priesthood, got married, and had two children. But he will always be remembered for his miracle worked in the Estudiantes stadium.

THE SENTENCE

The Iranians Mohammad Nosrati and Sheys Rezaei were two bold guys. On October 29, 2011, after Vashid Hashemian opened the scoring for Persepolis FC against Damash Gilan, their opponent in the Persian Gulf Cup, Nosrati had the great idea to approach the group hug that their teammates had formed and pinch Rezaei in the butt. The game, which took place at the Sardar Jangal Stadium, the home of Sports Club Damash Gilan, was drawn after three other goals. Three minutes from the end, when the match seemed to be destined for a 2-2 tie, Mohammad Nouri nailed the goal for the visitor team and the victory, and all the Persepolis players celebrated by forming a human pile next to the corner flag. There, Rezaei returned the affectionate pinch on the buttock to Nosrati. A few hours after the match ended, the joy of the Persepolis soccer players faded, especially that of the players with mischievous fingers: a Tehran court assessed the behavior of the scandalous players with excessive rigor and condemned them for inappropriate behavior to two months in prison and 74 lashes in public, the semi-official Iranian news agency *Fars* reported. For the court, the actions of Nosrati and Rezaei were considered a violation of public chastity. "The punishment of this crime is up to two months in prison and 74 lashes," said one of the magistrates, who said the episode was "very serious because their actions took place before the eyes of thousands of spectators and television cameras." At publication of this book, the two players had not returned to play in the local professional league. An exaggerated punishment that, without a doubt, seems excessive to Western eyes.

PAINFUL JOY

Situations such as those experienced by the Portuguese Paulo Diogo should make effusive scorers reconsider. A few stories earlier it was explained that FIFA included in their regulations a provision related to the players' clothing so that they did not use any object dangerous to themselves or to other players (including jewelry). On December 5, 2004, when this provision was not yet official, Servette Football Club Genève, last in the Swiss first division, defeated Fussballclub Schaffhausen, the next to last team, at home 2-1 and passed them in the standings. It was a very close match that could determine relegation, although the visiting team did not surrender and attacked in pursuit of the tie that would give them a bit of lift in their aspirations to reach the top flight. At 88 minutes, the speedy host attacker Diogo broke free, faced the rival goalkeeper, and with a precise right shot decided the crucial match. The Portuguese ran to his fans and jumped and hung on the boundary wire to join in the fans' celebration. But when he went down, his wedding ring—he had gotten married only a few days before—got hooked on the metal frame and cut off his finger. The scorer was transferred to a hospital in Zurich, where doctors tried in vain to reattach the appendage. As if the final amputation wasn't enough punishment, the Portuguese, on top of that, was given a yellow for excessive celebration.

It is often said that revenge will be terrible. Probably Thierry Henry can give lectures on the subject. On May 6, 2000, the

French forward scored two goals wearing the Arsenal FC shirt against Chelsea FC in one of the London derbies. After scoring the second goal, Henry ran to the corner flag and celebrated by kicking the flag. The flexible rod, like a fierce kick, bounced back and hit him hard in the face! The Frenchman was attended by the doctors of the "Gunners" and continued on the field, although somewhat dizzy. One positive was that those two goals were enough for a vital 2 to 1 triumph. The negative, in addition to the painful bruise, was that Henry received a yellow card from the severe referee Mike Reed.

One who suffered a damned celebration though completely blameless was the Argentine Martin Palermo. On November 29, 2001, Palermo, who wore the Villarreal C.F. shirt, scored the equalizer against Levante Unión Deportiva for the Copa del Rey. The attacker approached the stands to share his joy with a handful of fans of the "yellow submarine" who had traveled to the stadium City of Valencia, when the unforeseen happened: The wall that separated the fans from the field collapsed on Palermo's right leg, causing a double fracture of the tibia and fibula. The wall narrowly missed other Villarreal players who had approached the Argentine to congratulate him. "If three thousand people had gathered against that fence, the tragedy would have been much greater," said Romanian forward Gheorghe Craioveanu, who was almost hit by the wall. Because of this mishap, Palermo was inactive for more than four months.

On April 18, 1993, Arsenal FC and Sheffield Wednesday FC were drawing 1-1 at Wembley Stadium, the distinguished scene of the Football League Cup final. At 68 minutes, Englishman Paul Merson escaped free down the left and launched a cross that the Northern Irishman Stephen Morrow pushed to the net to score.

The scoreboard was not modified, and, with the referee's Allan Gunn final whistle, Arsenal celebrated a new title. While Morrow celebrated in front of his fans, the gigantic defender Tony Adams, captain of the "Gunners," ran 50 yards and tried to lift the hero on his shoulders with great force...and much ineptitude. The scorer fell backwards and fractured his right arm. Morrow missed the rest of the season but not the celebration, since he demanded that the team doctors apply a sling so he didn't miss the victory lap.

In Brazil, Saulo, keeper of Sport Club do Recife, was not satisfied with the meager 1-1 that, on the night of January 31, 2011, was achieved at home, Ilha do Retiro, against Associação Acadêmica e Desportiva Vitória das Tabocas, the worst team of the Pernambuco Championship. Already in added time, the referee Emerson Sobral granted a free kick to Recife next to the right corner of the rival area. The goalkeeper came out like an arrow toward the penalty box and asserted his 6-and-a-half-foot height to head a precise cross by Carlinhos Bala into the net. While about 20,000 people were delirious with elation, Saul ran to join the joy of their fans, but stepped badly and fell awkwardly behind the defeated goal. The bad step destroyed the anterior cruciate ligament of his right knee and kept him from playing for six months. While the goalie was removed on a stretcher, his position under the posts was put in the hands of Carlinhos Bala, barely 5.4 feet high. The small midfielder proved to be as skilled with his hands as he was with his feet and, with a couple of brave dives, kept his goal unbeaten until the end.

Another player who destroyed the ligaments of his knee was Bermudian Leonard Shaun Goater. In October 2002, at St. Andrew's Stadium in Birmingham City FC, the forward had no better idea than to celebrate a goal by his teammate Nicolas

Anelka with a kick against billboard. But Goater miscalculated his kick and his knee burst against the hard aluminum frame of the panel. Goater paid for his foolishness with two months of convalescence, a very cheap penalty for a reoffender: A few years earlier, in 1998, the attacker had decorated a goal with an intrepid somersault that culminated in fracturing one of his arms.

Something more spectacular, although in the same vein, was the intrepid pirouette of Celestine Babayaro. In 1997, the Nigerian celebrated a goal by Chelsea FC in an innocuous preseason game against weak Stevenage FC with an unnecessary somersault that led to a bad fall and a fracture that had him stopped, and standing, for several months.

However, the winner goes to the Argentine Fabián Espíndola of the American club Real Salt Lake. On September 7, 2008, five minutes into a league game against the Los Angeles Galaxy, which had not yet offered goals to the spectators who had arrived at Utah's Rio Tinto stadium, Espíndola pulled a powerful right shot that was nailed next to the left post of visiting keeper Steve Cronin. Happy for his achievement, the Argentine rehearsed a risky somersault that ended in a terrible landing. The blow caused a severe sprain in the left ankle, which kept off the field for two months. Espíndola left the game immediately and was replaced by the Armenian Yura Movsisyan, and while he was assisted by the doctors within inches of the line of the sideline, he learned that, following an offside by his partner Kyle Beckerman, his beautiful goal had been declared invalid.

FRIENDS ARE FRIENDS

In September of 1996, the passionate celebration that goalkeeper Leonardo Canales and defender Carlos Soto engaged in when Hector Cabello got the winning goal for Club de Deportes Coquimbo Unido in a first division match caused a major stir in Chile. Especially because the goalkeeper and the defender were part of Club Deportivo Provincial Osorno, the rival of Coquimbo that afternoon! The two players were immediately separated from the squad and subjected to a rigorous investigation. Wanted dead or alive by the furious Osorno fans, Canales and Soto had to escape from the city in the middle of the night. But, before escaping, they justified themselves for the unusual reaction: They assured everyone that they maintained an ironclad friendship with Cabello, which had been formed when the three had played together on other teams.

PIE-SMACKED

Goodison Park was boiling. The fourth round of the FA Cup had decided that the derby would be played in Liverpool, and, on January 24, 1981, Everton imposed home condition by winning 1-0. In the 15th minute of the second half, quick forward Eamon O'Keefe sailed to the left and delivered a precise cross to Imre Varadi which placed him comfortably between the desperate defenders and goalkeeper Ray Clemence; he managed to score easily. Varadi ran to the stand (which at that time was separated from the field by a fence) to celebrate with his fans, forgetting that, for the fiery match, that sector had been assigned to supporters of Liverpool FC, who were boiling with anger over the defeat that eliminated their beloved club from the competition. The gesture, although involuntary, threw fuel on the fire. Varadi only noticed his mistake when his face was inches from the fence, too late to elude a small bit of meat pie that was thrown at him by a furious "red" fan. "I was so euphoric that I ran to the grandstand that was full of Liverpool fans. Someone threw a pie that hit me squarely in the face; I can still taste it," Varadi recalled years later, with a smile and a bit of nostalgia for the delicious celebration.

DEVIL'S AFTERNOON

The afternoon of October 26, 1986, could not have been worse for Club Atlético Independiente. That day, the "red devils" received the modest Racing of the city of Córdoba for the Argentine first division tournament at home and, what in the papers seemed a comfortable and inconsequential victory, became slowly a real tragedy. Ten minutes into the second half, with the scoreboard still blank, referee Aníbal Hay ejected the greatest Red star, Ricardo Bochini, for protesting. Seventeen minutes later, the Cordoba goalkeeper Manuel Serrano stopped Gerardo Reinoso from the penalty spot. A quarter of an hour later, Independiente defender Juan Carlos Erba scored the only goal of the game, but in his own goal. And to round off one of the worst days of his life, just one minute from the end, the goalie Luis Islas collided with the rival striker Carlos Pajurek and suffered a double fracture of the fibula and tibia, an injury that forced him to remain out of the game for more than six months. As is often said, it was just a devil's afternoon.

HONEST BRIBERY

The president of a Croatian first division club admitted in August 2002 to bribing a referee "to ensure he did his job correctly." The "honorable" boss, Stjepan Spajic, head of Hrvatski Dragovoljac, handed over 10,000 euros to referee Ivan Katusa before the match with Slaven Belupo. But as Hrvatski fell 2 to 1 and was relegated, Spajic faced Katusa in the locker room and demanded the return of the money "because his refereeing was everything but honest." The man in black agreed. After the unusual case was brought to light by the press, the Croatian Disciplinary Committee suspended the executive for two years, and the referee for life, who learned that you can't have the cake and eat it too.

RED-CARDED TWICE...
IN THE SAME MATCH!

Clube Atlético Mineiro de Belo Horizonte, unbeaten in group 3 of the initial round of the Copa Libertadores—though without having yet won—was winning comfortably against the Paraguayan club Olimpia in Puerto Sajonia on March 16, 1972. Ronaldo (Ronaldo Gonçalves Drumond, no relation to the two outstanding players who would arrive decades later, Ronaldo Luiz Nazário de Lima and Ronaldo "Ronaldinho" of Assis Moreira), at 9 minutes, and Dario (Dario José dos Santos, a picturesque forward known as "Dada Maravilha," who would play on the Brazilian team that would be crowned World Cup champions in Mexico 1970) at 12, gave Mineiro a comfortable advantage. The Paraguayan team reacted and, thanks to a controversial performance by the Chilean referee Lorenzo Cantillana, managed to tie it with a goal from Alcides Sosa at 18 minutes and Crispín Verza at 73 minutes. "The ref put his hand in our pockets and robbed us; the two Olympia goals were nothing but scandalous," complained Dario years later.

The Verza goal was the most questioned by the men of the "Rooster," as it had materialized after a presumably clear foul during the attack. "I asked Cantillana to call something for us, and he gave me a straight red," continued the author of Mineiro's second goal. This red card lit up the spirits of the visiting players, who tried to attack the referee and his Paraguayan colleagues, a fact that unleashed a tremendous brawl. Because of the rain of kicks and punches, Cantillana threw out two other Brazilian players, Ronaldo and Odair, and one of the host players, Verza. During the incidents, Dario approached his team's assistant, took off his "9" jersey and asked for another one with the number "15," which he put on before going back on the field. As soon as the match resumed, Atlético Mineiro, only one man down despite the three reds, went on the attack, and Dario was about to unbalance the score, but his shot hit the crossbar. After that play, the Olimpia defenders realized Dada Maravilha's trickery and informed the referee. The Chilean, upon discovering the scheme, approached Dario and showed him the red card again, nine minutes after his first dismissal! The striker didn't go out alone: Humberto Ramos and Romeu accompanied him after they attacked Cantillana. Thus, Atlético Mineiro, who was tied, lost the match by having just six players, one less than the minimum allowed to compete. Although it could be said that there were seven red-carded because Dario had been shown the red card twice.

FATHER AND SON

Umberto Carlomagno, 47, and Biagino Carlomagno, 18, father and son, share a passion for soccer and maintain a rivalry for being starting goalkeepers for Lagonegro, club of the Italian national amateur championship in which they play. They suffered one of their worst afternoons on Sunday when they allowed eight goals between them. Lagonegro played against Altamura, a team that beat them 8 to 0. The curious thing is that both Umberto and Biagino played for one half each, though the son did slightly better since he only allowed two goals to pass him. Umberto had retired from soccer nine years ago, but faced with the crisis the team was having, with injuries and the departure of players, was forced to return. This was record in the Italian news agency *ANSA*, dated April 8, 1998, and shows that unusual things can happen in the relationship between parents, children, and soccer.

THE SON PLAYS, THE FATHER GETS THE MONEY

A friendly played on August 16, 2006, between England and Greece was not just another game for goalkeeper Chris Kirkland from the Wigan Athletic Club. That day he debuted on the British team. Chris replaced Paul Robinson in the goal, and that day they won 4 to 0. It wasn't just another game for Chris' father, Eddie, either. The man not only had the great pleasure of seeing his son perform under the posts of his national team, but he also earned an extra reward. Twelve years earlier, Eddie had bet 100 pounds at the bookmaker company William Hill that his son (then 13) would play goalie for the English national team before turning 30. The prediction finally came true, and Eddie, who had a "sport" of 100 to 1, received 10,000 pounds.

THEY SCORE ON THE SON, THEY EJECT THE FATHER

The anxiety and the enormous expectation that filled the "Cemetery of the Elephants" on March 4, 1998, day of the debut of the Argentine club Colón de Santa Fe in the Copa Libertadores, didn't last long. The more than 40,000 people gathered at the Brigadier General Estanislao López Stadium went from elation to disappointment in just 25 minutes when Club Atlético River Plate opened the scoring that turned the sweet premiere into something bitter. The goal was of the rare kind: A ball from visiting defender Celso Ayala, that had started on a free kick from his own field, flew 75 yards, hit a hole in the neglected penalty box of the host team, and, after making an unpredictable and surprising movement, beat the stretched arms of goalkeeper Leonardo Diaz, who could do nothing to prevent it. Colón fell that night by 2 to 1, but the "Fishermen" club was not the only one who lost. The next day, the furious executives of the Santa Fe institution fired the grounds keeper in charge of maintaining the pitch, considering him responsible for the setback in the international premiere. The dismissed employee was Marcelino Díaz, and—bizarrely—he was the father of Leonardo, the Colón goalie!

BLUE BLURRED NUMBERS

To visit Boca on July 8, 1984, for the first division championship, the Atlanta club assistants had the great idea to take to the "Bombonera" only two sets of t-shirts, both blue with very fine yellow stripes. This measure surprised the people in charge of preparing the host team's uniform—two changes with the traditional blue and gold design—since it was expected that the "Bohemian" squad would come in with their traditional blue jersey with yellow vertical stripes. With this emergency in mind, the "Xeneizes" went to the field with white training shirts, but since they lacked the corresponding numbers from 2 to 11, the solution was to scribble them by hand with blue oil paint that was found "somewhere around there." Of course, as the game went on and the players began to perspire, those that at first seemed like numbers soon turned into fuzzy, illegible blue smudges that smeared the garments and backs of the Boca players. It was not necessary, therefore, that the visiting players use the man-to-man defense to make things sticky. Annoyed by the situation, at halftime, the home team got rid of the improvised jerseys and dressed in the traditional ones without caring too much about the colorful confusion between the teams.

FROM THE FIELDS OF WAR TO THE SOCCER FIELD

After the defeat of the Republicans in the Spanish Civil War, the Basque Isidro Lángara—a former member of his country's national team in the 1934 World Cup in Italy—landed in the port of Buenos Aires on the morning of May 21, 1939. Of course, the arrival of Lángara to the Río de la Plata was not a secret: At the same wharf, several leaders of the San Lorenzo de Almagro club waited for him, eager for the immigrant, owner of a brilliant record as a scorer, to join their ranks and turn around the adverse streak of five games played without victory. The Spaniard accepted the proposal of the Boedo men, and that same afternoon was taken to the now defunct stadium on Avenida La Plata—which was known as "the Gasometer"—to dress in the red and blue colors and go out to play against River Plate for the first division Argentine tournament. Although, when he put his feet on the grass, the striker didn't make a good impression on the local fans as he was quite fat and seemed slow and heavy. Still, the brave Basque won the nickname "idol" that same afternoon by scoring four goals on the "millionaires" in less than half an hour between the 7th and 35th minutes of the first half. With his excellent play, Lángara—who wore the San Lorenzo shirt until 1942, a period during which he scored 110 goals in 121 games and was never expelled—contributed to the blue-and-red team, becoming one of the favorites of the Spanish community in Argentina.

INDESTRUCTIBLE

Baron James Kirkpatrick starred in an episode that, although endorsed by different journalistic and literary chronicles, has certain elements that bring it closer to a legend than to true story. On March 23, 1878, the Wanderers FC and Royal Engineers AFC teams met at the Kennington Oval Stadium in London for the final of the FA Cup 1877/78. According to what was recorded in the media at the time, Wanderers' goalkeeper Kirkpatrick broke his arm after 19 minutes. Because the regulation at the time didn't allow substitutions, Kirkpatrick stayed in the goal through the entire match. Despite such a notable disadvantage, his team won by 3 to 1! Some accounts of dubious veracity claim that, even when pressed by the serious injury, Kirkpatrick tried several reckless and successful somersaults in defense of his goal. Perhaps the fracture was not so bad, or perhaps Kirkpatrick's deeds were the product of flattering reporters. It wouldn't be the first time such things happened, nor the last...

FOUR AGAINST ELEVEN

On November 29, 1908, one of the most extraordinary matches in the history of soccer was played. For the first division tournament in the city of Copenhagen, Østerbros Boldklub (ØB) received Fælledparken Boldklubben af 1893 (B93), champion of the previous season, on their home field. Actually, they did not receive the whole team. Due to a problem with the train that transported the majority of the visiting team, B93, at the time of the initial whistle, only had four players. The referee tried to cancel the match, but the captain of ØB, unmoved, authorized his opponent to start the game. The man imagined this would allow ØB to win their first match of the championship. The small group was distributed on the pitch, and, with a remarkable effort, managed to finish the first half just 4 to 0 in favor of ØB. At halftime, the rest of the B93 team arrived, and now eleven against eleven, managed to turn the result and win by 5 to 4. Thanks to that heroic and incredible victory, B93 achieved the back-to-back championship because they edged up by just one point over the squad that came second, Kjøbenhavns Boldklub. Østerbros Boldklub, meanwhile, finished last, without having won or tied a single game.

THANKS TO THE FANS

On March 26, 1994, Chacarita and Almagro met in San Martín for the Argentine Primera B Championship. As both institutions were dressed by the same brand of sportswear, Penalty, a cup was put into play which would showcase the winning team. The initiative had the approval of the two clubs. However, the moment the players stepped onto the field...surprise! The two squads came out in totally white outfits. To make matters worse, no one had foreseen such a mishap. After several minutes, a home supporter proposed a solution to overcome the unfortunate blunder: to borrow the traditional shirts of red, black, and white vertical stripes with the numbers stamped on the back from the fans. In the blink of an eye, garments were thrown from the stands to fall behind the goal—enough to form dozens of squads. Bringing the colors of their beloved team to the stadiums was evidence of the Chacarita fans' loyalty. A selection of "2" to "16" was quickly assembled and distributed among the players, who started the play after 22 minutes of delay. Finally, Chacarita won by 3 to 2, earning them the trophy. When the captain Sergio Lara approached the manager of Penalty to receive the prize...another surprise! The defender wore a shirt with the Taiyo brand, the previous sponsor of the Cemetery Keepers.

THE TWO GOALIES PELÉ AND DI STÉFANO

The cold statistic indicates that the magnificent Spanish-Argentine striker Alfredo di Stéfano scored 377 goals in 521 appearances wearing the colors of River Plate, Huracán, Millonarios of Colombia, Real Madrid, and Real Club Deportivo Español de Barcelona. In addition, he got another six in the same number of matches with the Argentine team, and another 23 in 31 appearances with the "furious" red shirt of Spain. What the numbers do not say is that when his talent was required for a completely different role on the field, the "Blonde Arrow" did not back down. On July 30, 1949, during a hot superclásico, with River and Boca in the last two places of the standings of the Argentine first division tournament, Di Stéfano had to replace Amadeo Carrizo for six minutes after the legendary keeper received a blow to the liver. With his bare hands and barely wearing a short-sleeved shirt, "the German," as he was called, kept all balls from entering his goal until the goalkeeper recovered, and both returned to their original positions. Finally, the millionaire squad prevailed by the minimum difference of 1-0. The designation of Di Stéfano was not accidental. In fact, he himself was responsible for clarifying on numerous occasions that his favorite position "was always the goal," and that he enjoyed playing there during training when, instead of rehearsing attacks, he put on his gloves.

Another great goalkeeper, the fabulous Edson Arantes do Nascimento, known as Pelé, had his glory afternoon as number

"1." Maybe the fact of having scored so many goals gave him skills to avoid the fall of his own goal. On January 19, 1964, in the semifinals of the Taça Brasil, Gremio was defeating Santos 3 to 1 at the Pacaembú of San Pablo until "the King" scored the three goals that turned the game around. Caring little about his feat, Pelé settled in the goal of the *santista* team when the Argentine referee Teodoro Nitti expelled goalkeeper Gilmar. With the same skill that he showed on the pitch when kicking the ball, the "10" made several spectacular saves that prevented the "Gaucho" draw and sealed the triumph for Santos. His remarkable conditions to guard the posts seem to have been inherited by his son "Edinho," who for several seasons wore the goalkeeper jersey of that club, although as a starter.

THE DAY THAT BRAZIL PLAYED WITH BOCA'S JERSEY

Brazil played the first edition of the Copa América in Buenos Aires in 1916 with a jersey made up of green and yellow vertical stripes. From 1919, the Brazilian squad wore white until the failure of the 1950 World Cup motivated the managers to change the national outfit. But before that, on January 3, 1937, in a new Copa América organized by Argentina, Brazil went out onto the pitch of Boca Juniors with their white uniform, and, to their surprise, Chile appeared in white, too. It was their distinctive tone—the red, it was said—that would become official a few years later in the 1940s. For the teams to differentiate themselves, a host club officer provided a set of jerseys and, for that one day, Brazil was "Xeneize." And it wasn't that bad. They won 6 to 4.

BREAD

On the night of October 19, 1983, at the Instituto de Córdoba stadium, the striker for San Lorenzo de Almagro, Walter Perazzo, could barely see the ball. Famished from missing the afternoon snack after taking a nap longer than he should, Perazzo didn't even have the strength to return to the locker room. The first half finished, and in the visitor's dressing room there was not even a candy to dull his hunger pains. Already in the second half, with the score 1-1 and blood pressure low, the attacker felt a blow to the back, followed by a shout: "You're starving of goals!" He turned around and saw a shiny loaf of bread, intact on the pitch, that had been thrown by a fan making fun of him. He didn't think twice; he broke it in two and ate it in two bites. With a full belly and a happy heart, Perazzo scored the second goal by the "saints," a great goal, and assisted two more goals for the Buenos Aires squad to win 4 to 1.

THE WARNING

Throughout a century and a half of soccer, several players, coaches, and even referees have died while intervening in a game, either by receiving a strong blow or by a heart disease. The death of the Cameroonian Marc-Vivien Foé is one of the most extraordinary for having occurred during a match for the FIFA Confederations Cup in June 2003 against Colombia. At 72 minutes, while the play was taking place in another part of the field, Foé collapsed on the grass after suffering a decompensation caused by a hypertrophic cardiomyopathy. The doctors tried to revive him for 45 minutes, but the African did not react. He had died in front of the television cameras that transmitted the dramatic event live to everyone.

Another exceptional case involved defender Goran Tunjic. In May 2010, the clubs NK Mladost-Ždralovi and Hrvatski Sokol played in an intense 0-0 for the fifth division of the Croatian championship. Halfway through the second half, when the visiting squad was pelting the NK Mladost box, Tunjic fell while fighting for the ball with a rival. When the player didn't get up, referee Marko Maruncek approached him, and, assuming that he was wasting time, took out the yellow card. Despite the warning and the reproaches of the referee, the defender, 32 years old, remained on the ground, immobile. Seeing that the man still didn't react, Maruncek, on the verge of panic, ordered the entrance of the medical team, who discovered that the player was, in fact, dead. Maruncek suspended the match and, of course, didn't write down the yellow on his report.

SCARVES

After passing through Chacarita Juniors—the team with which he achieved first division promotion in 194—and Vélez Sarsfield, center forward Marcos Aurelio transferred with his Vélez companions Miguel Rugilo and Ángel Fernández to the Mexican club León in the middle of a massive exodus of Argentine players to Mexican soccer in 1944. There he had a coach who used a complex method based on different colored handkerchiefs to give instructions to his players. If the manager waved a blue one, everyone had to go on the attack. On the other hand, if he exhibited a green one, the eleven players had to defend. And if the chosen handkerchief was red, a player had to keep the ball. The new strategy was put into practice in a first division game, but things didn't go well at all. Even though the trail-blazing coach changed colors, the goals for the rivals came one after the other. With the match at an unfavorable 5-1, Aurelio approached the bench and, addressing the coach, asked: "What do you think if you take out a white handkerchief and we surrender?"

"HOSTS" IN ANOTHER COUNTRY

On March 3, 2014, a unique event occurred in the history of the Copa Libertadores: A team that played as a visitor abroad brought more fans to the stadium than the host playing in its own country. This unusual situation took place when Arsenal Football Club—a club that had been established less than 60 years before, with a poor fan base but with excellent sporting results since the 21st century—received on its home field, "Julio Humberto Grondona," the Club Atlético Peñarol, for group 8 of the first phase of the continental tournament. That afternoon, some 5,000 people entered the small stadium located in the town of Sarandí in the suburbs of the city of Buenos Aires. More than 3,000 were fans of Peñarol, who outnumbered the always small fanbase of Arsenal. Until that moment, the times in which a visiting team had surpassed the hosts in attendance, had only happened in duels between institutions of the same nation.

HOT WATER SHOWERS

The wives and girlfriends of the soccer players who participated in the Exeter and District Sunday League were shocked when they learned that a female referee, Janet Fewings, was showering after the games...with the players! At 41, this mother of four children undressed and took her post-match bath quietly with the boys. "In the stadiums of small clubs, there are no separate showers for women and men," the referee explained when the scandal broke out in mid-1996. "I have seen everything before, and I assure you that, often, it is not the most beautiful sight in the world," she replied without embarrassment to the complaints of the jealous women. Throughout an extensive career of more than one hundred refereed matches, Fewings had change in kitchens, bars, and even in a broom closet. Fed up, one day she decided to get into the dressing room of one of the two teams and, without any shame, cooled off with the naked players. Interviewed by the English newspaper *The Mirror*, one of those players commented with humor: "First I was shocked to see a naked woman in the shower next door, but then I thought it was the best result of the whole season." Janet also had a humorous take on the case: "It's better than changing with the brooms, unless one of the boys has drunk a lot the night before."

THE BALL BOY SCORER

Throughout soccer's history and, especially, in this chapter, strange goals of all kinds have been recorded. On December 3, 2006, during a match of the Copa de la Federación de São Paulo, one of the most unexpected occurred. The goal was scored by one of the ball boys! That day, at the Leonidas Camarinha stadium, FC Sorocaba was winning 1-0 against Associação Esportiva Santacruzense. Just one minute from the end, host forward Samuel shot from the right in search of the tie, but the ball went very close to the post and fell at the feet of a child who officiated as a ball boy. The boy quickly got onto the field and kicked the ball to the back of the net. Sorocaba's goalkeeper, Eduardo, took the ball out of the net, placed it in a corner spot of the goalkeeper's area, and prepared to take the goal kick, but incredibly referee Silvia Regina de Oliveira asked for it and took it to the center spot of the field, while with her whistle she validated the incredible goal. The match ended even, and in spite of the complaints and the videos presented by the Sorocaba leaders, the Federação Paulista de Futebol informed that it was legally impossible to annul the irregular goal because it was validated by the referee. Throwing more fuel onto the fire, Samuel acknowledged to the press that the goal had been unlawful but said that "if the referee decided it was a goal, it was a goal." An example of very unfair play.

NOT EVEN TWELVE!

On September 10, 2006, Morón faced Brown de Adrogué on their home field for the B Metropolitan Division of Argentina. After only 16 minutes, Marcelo Vega got injured and, while he was being treated, the doctor signaled the coach of the hosts Morón, Salvador Daniele to replace him. With a corner kick against them, Daniele made Diego Perotti, a sub, come in so that they didn't defend with a man down. But Vega was still in the field, and he ran to his penalty box to assist in the clearance. Neither the referee Cristian Faraoni nor his assistant Jose Mendoza were aware of the issue and ordered the corner to be taken even though Morón had twelve soccer players on the field! Adrián Zen Bonacorsi sent a curling shot that wasn't handled well by goalkeeper Maximiliano Gagliardo and went in next to the far post. While the visitors were celebrating, the referee noticed his horrendous mistake and ordered Vega to leave the field. With eleven again, Morón scored the equalizer at 23 minutes in the second half, thanks to a formidable shot from Ceferino Denis. At 32 minutes, Morón was again numerically superior after Gonzalo González received the red card, but they again failed to take advantage and could not gain an advantage, and the match ended 1-1.

THE ORGY

Israel had achieved a remarkable second place in their qualifying group for Euro 2000, which took place in the Netherlands and Belgium. The team, geographically in Asia, but playing in Europe because of their political situation with their neighbors, ended up behind Spain, which classified for the continental tournament, but ended ahead of Austria, Cyprus, and San Marino. In the playoff, Israel had to face Denmark in a home-and-away duel in pursuit of a bid that had never been achieved in its history. Before the big event, the team settled in Tel Aviv for the first match played on November 13, 1999, at the Ramat Gan stadium. However, the night before the game, four of the starters were "preparing" for the match with prostitutes until sunrise. The revelry—journal articles reported that several used condoms were found in a room—had dire consequences: the Danes crushed the Israelis 5 to 0. In the remaining game in Copenhagen, Denmark sealed their qualification with a 3-0 win that determined a global 8-0. The federation, aware of the singular event, decided to dismiss the four partiers and the coach, Schlomo Scherf. However, they never did mete out the punishment. After a few weeks, the players involved published an apology letter in a local newspaper, vowing never to repeat the incident and donated about $19,000 to a children's charity. A very expensive orgy—for which they had to pay twice.

LUCKY IN MISFORTUNE

Brazilian striker Thiago Neves Augusto has a bittersweet record: He is the only player who scored three goals in a Copa Libertadores final match. But, despite his efficiency in the net, his team, Fluminense Football Club, wasn't champion! This particular case occurred in the 2008 edition, when the tri-color team of Rio de Janeiro faced the Universidad Deportiva Liga de Quito in the culminating match. Thiago Neves made one of the two goals for Cariocas in the first leg match, although the Ecuadorian club won 4 to 2. In the rematch, in the Maracanã stadium, the attacker had his famous hat trick, and "Flu" won 3 to 1. In the deciding shots from the penalty spot, the visiting goalkeeper Jose Cevallos rejected three shots—one by poor Thiago Neves—for the Liga to be crowned as the first club in their country to win the Libertadores.

FORWARD AND SUBSTITUTE GOALKEEPER

Since childhood, Irish Niall Quinn was noted for his skills with his feet...and also his hands. During his childhood in Dublin, he excelled in Gaelic football, a mixture of rugby and soccer that is practiced with a round but heavier ball than its soccer cousin, and the goals are in the shape of "H," and the scoring team earns one or three points, depending on whether the ball passes under or above the crossbar. Upon entering adolescence, the young man decided to become a soccer player and enlisted in the Dublin club Manortown United FC. However, he was faced with a huge dilemma: to be a striker or goalkeeper. He was just as good in one position as he was in the other. Advised by his coach, he chose to become center forward, a good choice because, in a few months, his masterful goals helped him to cross the Irish Sea to enlist in the prestigious ranks of Arsenal FC club in London. In the first division of England, Quinn scored 141 goals in 475 games with the "Gunners," Manchester City FC and Sunderland AFC. With the Irish team he added another 21 goals in 92 games. But the prolific harvest of goals never put out his love for placing himself under the posts. In training, Quinn used to put on gloves to break the habit. His excellent ability as a goalkeeper allowed English coach Jack Charlton to bring only two goalkeepers to the 1990 World Cup in Italy (Pat Bonner and Gerald Peyton), unusual at a time when the teams allowed 22 players and not 23, as has happened ever since Korea-Japan 2002. Charlton (champion in the 1966 World Cup as a player) did not need to use Quinn as goalkeeper, but he enjoyed a goal against Holland, at the Renzo Barbera Stadium in Palermo.

Who did need the safe hands of the attacker was Manchester City coach Peter Reid, who on April 20, 1991, against Derby County FC, used a setup similar to the green national team, but a bit more risky. With the Irish player on the field, he sat five field players (by then the maximum number of substitutes allowed) on the bench. The sky-blue squad—the hosts at Maine Road—won 1-0 thanks to a left-foot shot from Quinn himself from outside the box that was nailed down on Martin Taylor's left post. Shortly thereafter, visiting striker Dean Saunders was brought down by goalkeeper Tony Coton: penalty and red card for the "1" (it is fair to note here that Coton debuted in first division play with Birmingham City FC against Sunderland on December 27, 1980; the first ball he touched was a John Hawley penalty kick, which he deflected masterfully). Without a substitute goalkeeper, the goal scorer went to the goal with the gloves and the green goalkeeper jersey of his partner to face Saunders, a clear example of "they do it to me, I do it to them." The attacker of "the Rams" took a shot to the right corner that the Irishman blocked masterfully with his left hand. Manchester City won that afternoon 2-1, aided by Quinn's fantastic feat. With that defeat, Derby was relegated.

SPECIAL GOALIE SUBSTITUTIONS

In September 2005, the Sunnana SK was not in the best condition to receive Burea IK for the championship of the fourth division of Sweden. The goalkeeper was injured, and work commitments prevented his substitute from playing. In a fit of despair, the club's president, Sören Gustafsson, decided to summon Asa Berglund, the goalkeeper of the Sunnana women's team. Gustafsson examined the national regulations with a magnifying glass and confirmed that there was no regulation against a woman playing on a men's team. He did find that it was forbidden for a man to play on a women's squad. On the afternoon of the match, the Sunnana home field was overrun with 400 spectators—their average was 200—all there to see Asa's performance among the men. Burea finally prevailed 2 to 1, and according to the news, the goalie bore no responsibility for either of the two received. What was not reported is whether the goalie used the same locker room as her companions.

A similar case, though not for the gender issue, occurred in Romania on November 2, 2002. The leader of the first division championship, Rapid Bucharest, was suddenly without goalkeepers—all were injured—to face off against the Arges Pitesti. With no other options, the coach summoned the vice president of the Rapid, Razvan Lucescu, age 33, who had retired few years before, to play. The executive, who had had a distinguished career, proved more than capable, and his team won 1-0.

INTOLERANCE

On August 22, 2002, the Brazilian referee Jenhins Barbosa dos Santos took to the field to officiate a match of the under-15 championship of the state of São Paulo with his whistle, his yellow and red cards, his watch...but not with a drop of tolerance or common sense. During the game, Barbosa dos Santos forced a defender from Botafogo to repeat a throw-in several times, but as the young man didn't do it as FIFA says to, he gave him a yellow card. The boy in question, Waine Raphael Araújo, 15 years old, could hardly carry out the deed "with both hands," as the FIFA regulations points out, because he was handless from birth. To make matters worse, when Zito, the Botafogo coach, complained about what he considered intolerant and cruel behavior, he was expelled by the pitiless man in black. The situation outraged Araújo's relatives, who had to endure the sad situation from the stands. But, right after the match, they filed a lawsuit with the local authorities on the grounds that the boy had been subjected to discrimination, and the club filed a complaint with the Football Federation of the State of São Paulo.

THE BROTHERHOOD

The Argentine national team has a record that is unlikely to be beaten: having started four brothers among their eleven players in the same match. They were Jorge, Eliseo, Ernesto, and Alfredo Brown, who on July 9, 1908, formed the national squad that, in a friendly match, defeated by 3 to 2 a team of Rio players in Rio de Janeiro, Brazil. The Browns, legendary heroes of Argentine soccer and of Scottish descent, had a fifth brother, Carlos, who also wore the sky-blue-and white jersey, but never with more than two of his brothers. The five Browns did come together with the red-and-white colors of Alumni, but they didn't manage to play all together for the national team.

This, as was said, was unlikely to be broken, but it was matched on June 5, 2012, when the Tahitian national team came out to face the Vanuatu squad at the Lawson Tama Stadium in the city of Honiara (Solomon Islands) for the Oceania qualifiers for the 2014 World Cup in Brazil. On that day, the team included Lorenzo, Alvin, Jonathan, and Teaonui Tehau. The quartet was repeated three days later against Solomon Islands, although for a few minutes, because Teaonui entered at the 75th minute to replace Steevy Chong Hue. The same happened on September 12 against New Caledonia (Teaonui replaced Stanley Atani). However, the greatest achievement of this family occurred on June 1, 2012, when Tahiti faced Samoa. The four Tehau brothers scored goals in the 10-1 victory. Lorenzo scored four goals, Alvin two, and

Jonathan two others. The ninth goal was achieved by Teaonui, who had joined Alvin. Steevy Chong Hue had the "honor" of getting the only goal that was not part of the family. The brothers scored several more goals, but in the continental final stage, the efficiency of the Tehau brothers wasn't enough, and Tahiti ended up far from New Zealand, the winner of the area that contested the playoff against the fourth team of CONCACAF, Mexico.

THE FLYING MOTORCYCLE

At the beginning of May 2001, Inter Milan defeated Atalanta at home 3 to 0 with goals from Italian Christian Vieri and Uruguayan Alvaro Recoba. Despite the comfortable triumph in the Serie A, the local "ultras" were particularly belligerent, and they began throwing all kinds of projectiles toward the pitch below from the second level of the San Siro stadium. And the expression "all kinds" is not exaggerated, because one of the objects thrown from those stands was a moped! According to the police, the small motorcycle was transported by a ramp to the top of the grandstand, and from there it was thrown onto the field. What the law enforcement agencies didn't explain is how they allowed the moped to get that far.

DEFLATED VICTORY

In March of 2000, in Brazil, Portuguesa was in complete control against Matonese at home during the second round of the Paulista Championship. Six minutes into the first half, and with the host team up early 1 to 0, Evandro received a ball from Marco Goiano, passed it to Betinho, and the attacker fired a missile that stuck in the net. Despite the celebrations of the Portuguesa eleven and his fans, the referee Vladimir Vassoler—from the field side of Matonese, because in the Paulista Championship they were trying out having two referees—refused to validate the goal, called for a drop ball, and ran to take the ball shot by Betinho. The spectators couldn't believe what they saw, but Vassoler showed the ball and sank his hand into it to demonstrate the reason for his decision: The ball had been punctured by the impact and deflated during its trip to the bottom of the net. Although he toured the entire field to show the fans what had happened, it didn't stop the fans from throwing insults at him. To make matters worse, Matonese reacted, and the match ended tied 2 to 2. Betinho? He had gone to the showers a while before, after being shown the red card for protesting.

THE PARDON

For the qualifiers for the England World Cup, Mexico and Costa Rica had to face each other in a final group stage of three that also included Jamaica. The mini-tournament began on April 25, 1965, with a 0-0 tie between the two squads. This match began with remarkable fellowship—the president of the visiting federation, Guillermo Cañedo, assured the press that he was surprised when the local fans "sang the Mexico anthem in the previous ceremony"—but, eventually, nerves typical of a virtual elimination diluted the camaraderie into a stream of kicks and punches. The episodes of violence in the second half forced the Canadian referee Raymond Morgan to eject the visitor Isidoro Díaz and the host Juan José Gámez for attacking each other.

On May 16, both teams met again at the stadium of the Mexican University City. The two had won all their games against the islanders, some by several goals, so that in this game of the brand-new CONCACAF (Confederation of North, Central American and Caribbean Association Football) would decide the winner who would then be traveling to England. At 16 minutes, the Mexican Ernesto Cisneros opened the scoring with a header after anticipating the false start of goalkeeper Emilio Sagot. The goal rekindled the embers of the first leg, which had not been completely extinguished. A minute after the goal, a clash between Ernesto Cisneros and the Costa Rican Alvaro MacDonald unleashed a pitched battle that involved all players on the field. After 18 minutes of punches and kicks, Morgan, the referee—who, curiously, was assisted by the Mexican Fernando Buergo and the Costa Rican Alfonso Benavides—decided to throw out Antonio Munguía and Carlos Quirós, two of the most warlike fighters. However, the FIFA observer, Englishman Jimmy McGuire, went over the authority of the referee to exonerate Munguía and Quirós and ordered them both to return to the pitch to play. "It was common sense to continue the match," McGuire explained to the press, after the final whistle, "the show had to continue because the public had paid to watch a soccer match. I believe I have done the right thing, without getting into the regulations. So, at least, I feel about it. I summoned the two captains and begged them to act cleanly and nobly; it was the best thing that could be done without harming anyone. There were so many kicks and blows that we did not know who the real culprits were. The majority fought in the fight and the majority deserved the ejection. If the game continued with ten men, the chivalry of the players would have disappeared, and this would have resulted in more unnecessary aggression."

After the violent interruption, the two teams continued with eleven protagonists. The scoreboard remained unchanged, and Mexico advanced to the World Cup after a game that had two ejections which, officially, never existed.

ALL WRONG

The Venezuelan goalkeeper Rafael Dudamel stood out for his excellent reflexes, great agility, and good foot skills. In addition to being spectacular under the posts, the goalkeeper was even the author of many goals, totaling 22 in twenty years of professional soccer, most of them from the penalty spot. One of his most famous goals occurred on September 10, 1996, when he scored a formidable free kick against the Argentine team for the 1998 World Cup qualifiers. But, on April 29, 2004, during the Copa Libertadores wild-card match between Barcelona Sporting Club of Ecuador and Unión Atlético Maracaibo of Venezuela, Dudamel took part in a nefarious incident.

At 84 minutes, the Ecuador team with a wide advantage by 5 to 1, the Bolivian referee René Ortubé called a penalty kick for Maracaibo. The goalkeeper ran to the rival area to execute the shot, but the Argentine striker Mariano Martínez and the Caribbean striker Giancarlo Maldonado stood in his way, both desiring to pick up the foul and get on the scoreboard. Although Uruguayan coach Jorge Siviero had appointed Maldonado, the number "one" moved his teammates to the side and shot the penalty kick, which was stopped by goalkeeper Geovanny Camacho. Because of his mistake, but much more because of his selfish attitude, Dudamel, harshly questioned by his comrades, decided to leave the field. No, it wasn't a substitution: He just went straight to the locker room, which forced the referee to red-card him for unsportsmanlike conduct. In addition, Siviero had to waste a sub to include his substitute goalkeeper, Tulio Hernandez, on the field. After the match, 6 to 1 in favor of Barcelona, the problems continued inside the Venezuelan dressing room. Dudamel, after coming to blows with Maldonado, decided to leave the team. "The best thing was to separate myself from the group to reflect upon my actions," he said. A few days later, he was already training with his new teammates from the Corporación Club Deportivo Tuluá of Colombia.

IN THE TWO GOALS

Many players have lived a bittersweet day after scoring two goals in the same match: one in favor of the team they represent, another against. Only two experienced such a day during a World Cup: the Dutchman Ernstus "Ernie" Brandts and the Croatian Mario Mandžukić. On June 21, 1978, at the CA River Plate stadium, the day that closed the semifinal group A, couldn't begin more inauspiciously for the Dutch defender of the "clockwork orange," who wore the white shirt that afternoon. At 18 minutes, Brandts tried to deactivate an attack commanded by Marco Tardelli and, when sweeping, not only sent the ball to the back of the net, but also fractured his goalkeeper Piet Schrijvers. At 5 minutes into the second half, Brandts went on the offensive, bent on regaining his honor. He went up the field and, after a rebound outside the "azzurri" box, nailed a ferocious shot into the right corner of the net against goalkeeper Dino Zoff. Arie Haan, with another tremendous shot from 30 meters that entered next to the left post, gave Holland the victory and the qualification to the final against Argentina.

On July 5, at the Luzhniki Olympic Stadium, Mandžukić opened the score of the Russian World Champion final against France with a bad header (i.e., one he put into his own goal). The Croatian forward had a little revenge in the second half when he took advantage of an error by French goalkeeper Hugo Lloris.

223

Unfortunately for Mandžukić, this success wasn't enough to reverse a *bleu* victory by 4 to 2.

On Saturday, September 25, 1976, for the English Second Division, Sheffield United FC faced Blackburn Rovers FC at home, and Plymouth Argyle FC hosted Bolton Wanderers FC. Both matches finished 1-1. And in both matches, the two goals came from the same men, curiously from the host team: Colin Franks and Paul Mariner, respectively.

With some variant in the score, this particular coincidence occurred in the 14th round of the Argentine Clausura Championship of 1997, in the meetings between Club Gimnasia y Esgrima La Plata 3-C and CA Banfield 2-CA. Gimnasia y Esgrima de Jujuy 2 played in La Plata, and CA Banfield 2-CA Platense 2 played at Banfield's stadium. Guillermo Sanguinetti and Néstor Craviotto—also players for the host squads—scored the two goals with an another fun coincidence: Both played in the same position, right back, and with the same number on their back, "4."

Back in England, on October 5, 1974, the London stadium White Hart Lane was the scene of a hilarious situation. In just 20 minutes, Tottenham Hotspur FC captain Mike England twice beat his own goalkeeper, Pat Jennings, in favor of their rival, Burnley FC: first, by pushing Ian Brennan's cross into the back of the net, and then, by deflecting a shot from Paul Fletcher. The home team got one back through John Pratt and, eight minutes from the end, the embarrassed Mike England went to the rival penalty box, headed a corner kick by Jimmy Neighbour, and equalized the match. But what had started as an unlucky afternoon for Tottenham ended in a real nightmare. On the final play, visiting striker Leighton James fired his last shot into Jennings' goal. The ball changed its trajectory by hitting John Pratt and ending inside the goal, giving Burnley the victory. An unfortunate Tottenham match, which scored five goals to fall 2-3.

However, in this category, the gold medal was won by Northern Irishman Chris Nicholls from Aston Villa FC, who on March 20, 1976, in a match for the English first division against Leicester City FC, scored four goals. The match ended...2-2!

SMOKE BREAK

On May 22, 1974, the Argentine national team visited the England team in the traditional Wembley stadium during a preparatory tour for the World Cup that would take place in Germany less than a month later. In that match, striker René Houseman, who was nicknamed "El Loco" (the Crazy Man), was the protagonist of a very funny episode. Shortly after the second half started, coach Vladislao Cap decided to make a change and shouted at Houseman to start warming up. The coach waited a little while and soon realized that there was no movement around the bench. He looked closely and discovered, horrified, that Houseman was not getting ready or sitting between the substitutes. Cap, on the verge of a heart attack, consulted his assistant coaches José Varacka and Víctor Rodríguez and the other players, but nobody knew anything. A few minutes later, "Crazy Man" appeared, finally. He had been in the locker room smoking a cigarette! Houseman came in for Miguel Brindisi and started the play that ended in the penalty kick with which Mario Kempes tied the match 2 to 2.

UNUSUAL DOUBLE

Rarely has a similar blooper been seen in an official match like the one that happened on February 24, 1996, during the Pre-Olympic tournament played in the Argentine city of Mar del Plata. At 27 minutes into the second half, with 3-2 for Venezuela on the scoreboard, the Paraguayan referee Epifanio Gonzalez gave a penalty shot to Ecuador that gave the team hope to tie the match. Defender Segundo Matamba, in charge of the shot, placed the ball in its spot, took a run, and with a left-foot cross beat the Venezuelan goalkeeper Rafael Dudamel. The referee, instead of pointing to the center of the field, ordered the repetition of the penalty because, when kicking, Matamba's boot had come off and had followed the path of the ball to the back of the net—something that, in the neighborhood playing fields, the boys often jokingly call a "double goal." Matamba fired again and, although you may not believe it, the shoe came off again, but this time with a small difference in trajectory. The ball bounced off the crossbar and was rejected by the defense; the footwear, for its part, hit the left post of the Venezuelan goal. The referee, in this case, considered the goal valid—which was fine since the irregularity had not been caused by the goalkeeper or his defense—and the match continued on. There was room for another double: two balls into the Ecuadorian net, which rounded off a remarkable triumph of 5 to 2 for the Venezuelan national team.

GOALIE, TAKE CARE OF YOUR SHOE!

The book, *Curiosities of Football,* by the English journalist Jonathan Rice, rescues a juicy anecdote about Robert Kelly, forward for the club Burnley FC in the 1920s. As the owner of a very strong kick, Kelly was in charge of implementing the penalties. On one occasion, when taking a shot from the twelve yards, the attacker took a huge run, kicked, and shot the ball at full speed, but his shoe shot forward with the ball. The rival goalkeeper dove and caught, not the ball, but the boot! The ball, meanwhile, went straight into the net, helped by the confusion of the goalkeeper in deciding between the two leathers. Contrary to what happened in the preceding story, in Mar del Plata, here the ref was wrong for authorizing the goal.

RED FOR THE FANS

It is said that there are no worse *barrabravas,* or hooligans, than the parents of soccer players, especially during children and youth matches. In addition to pressuring their children to achieve victory at any price, adults forget the context of the game, and, instead of being a good example, teach the boys the most varied range of insults, often complemented by boxing or wrestling scenes. In November 1995, referee Dave Warwick had to resort to extremes to protect the eleven-year-old boys from Gillway Boys FC and Bedworth United FC, who were facing each other by the Tamworth Junior League of the county of Staffordshire in the center of England. Fed up with about twenty dads and moms attacking each other and mistreating the players with their foul language, Warwick stopped the play, pulled out his red card, and showed it to the two fanbases. The referee warned them that if they did not withdraw from around the field, he would suspend the match. The parents went away to the parking lot, and the boys, free of the verbal tirades, finished the game in absolute peace and harmony.

WELL-PAID REVENGE

The soccer players from the Bolivian club The Strongest were livid, and not only because of the 4 to 0 they had just suffered that February 15 against the Sociedade Esportiva Palmeiras in the stadium "Parque Antarctica" of San Pablo, in the opening of group 7 of the first round of the 2000 Copa Libertadores. The Andean players went berserk after discovering that, while their own goal was attacked again and again, on the other side of the field, the goalkeeper of the Brazilian team, Marcos Roberto Silveira Reis, drank coffee in the most relaxed manner, lying against one of his poles. The Bolivian players acknowledged their own shortcomings in reaching the Palmeiras penalty box that night, but they felt that Marcos' attitude was, at the very least, in bad taste. Enraged, the Andeans left Brazil thirsting for revenge at the height of La Paz, and ruminating on that famous proverb that guarantees that "time makes everything right." On April 6, Palmeiras traveled to the Bolivian capital to face The Strongest at the Hernando Siles Coliseum, some 12,100 feet above sea level. There, the striped squad could retaliate with four goals of their own against the cocky Marcos. Each one of the goals by Antonio Vidal González, Sandro Coelho, Daniel Delfino, and Josué "Índio" Ferreira Filho was celebrated in the same effusive way: with the group of soccer players who had participated in the play sitting inside of the penalty box of the goalkeeper from São Paulo, pretending to drink a cup of coffee. Despite this 4-2 victory, the Bolivian team failed to qualify for the second phase of the Cup. But, at least, they managed to sweeten the bitter taste that lingered after their trip to Brazil.

I'M NOT LEAVING

Oldham Athletic AFC never won the first division tournament in England but was very close to achieving it in the 1914/15 season. The title escaped them by only one point and was held by Everton FC, thanks to a strange situation. On April 3, 1915, Oldham Athletic, leader of the championship, traveled to the Ayresome Park stadium to face Middlesbrough FC, which was very close to the relegation zone. However, that afternoon Boro was very inspired, and 10 minutes into the second half they were ahead 4-1, thanks to a penalty shot converted by Walter Tinsley after a strong foul by the defender from the away team, Billy Cook. Seconds after the fourth goal, Cook committed another hard foul, and ref Harry Smith ejected him from the pitch. But the defender, enraged by what he considered a subjective decision, refused to leave the field. Faced with Cook's stubborn attitude, Smith suspended the match. Days later, the Football Association gave the match to Middlesbrough and suspended Cook for twelve months. Without one of their most important players, Oldham lost the victorious streak and handed over the title to Everton.

MOTIVATED

Vila Nova Futebol Clube had fallen to the Third Division of Brazil, and their situation was alarming. Before the beginning of the 1996 season, one of the directors, owner of a luxurious "romantic" hotel in the city of Goiania, who was also a sponsor of the team, proposed to give a free night, including champagne, to anyone chosen by the fans as the best player of each game. The proposal renewed the vigor of the boys. Vila Nova went undefeated to win the Série C Brazilian Championship.

In mid-2008, in the city of Copenhagen, the president of FC København of the Danish first division, Flemming Østergaard, offered his players two "porn specials" for each victory. The films were produced and distributed by the company BN Agentur, sponsor of the club. København not only retained the title, but also won 23 of the 33 matches played. As a reward, each player received 46 erotic videos. They didn't have enough hands...to take the prize home!

Nigeria did not get off to a good start in the African Cup of Nations 2013, which was played in South Africa. Their first two matches in Group C were two 1-1 draws with Burkina Faso and Zambia. With the team at serious risk of being eliminated, a particular message of encouragement came from Lagos: the Nigerian Association of Prostitutes offered the players a week of free sex if the situation was reversed, and they won the tournament. The response from the boys was extraordinarily positive as they went on to beat Ethiopia 2-0 in the last match of the first phase, Côte d'Ivoire 2-1 in the quarterfinals, Mali 4-1 in the semifinal, and Burkina Faso 1-0 in the final. It was not known if the "Super Eagles" accepted their prize, but there is no doubt that the stimulus was very effective.

EXPENSIVE GOALS

The official debut of the French team was a vibrant three-goal draw against their Belgian counterpart in Brussels on May 1, 1904. In contrast, the first "international" match played by a French team took place a year earlier, on April 26, when a team consisting of eleven Parisian players dressed in red faced a set of English stars dressed in white. That afternoon there was no draw, although both squads were very happy at the Parc des Princes of the City of Lights: the away team for having imposed their superiority by an unobjectionable 11-0. The hosts were happy also, because 984 people had paid to see the match. The ticket sales amounted to 1,246 francs, a fortune in those times!

On November 22, 2009, the White Hart Lane stadium was the scene of the second biggest win in the English Premier League: Tottenham Hotspur FC, 9, against Wigan Athletic FC,1 (the record was, at the close of this edition, Manchester United FC, 9, Ipswich Town FC, 0, in 1995). The heavy defeat caused the coach of the away team, Roberto Martínez, to resign and an unusual gesture by the humiliated players: At the initiative of their captain, the Dutch Mario Melchiot, the players decided to return the amount of tickets for the 400 fans who had traveled from Wigan—a locality of Great Manchester, in the northwest of England—to Tottenham's home, in London. "We are a group of professionals who feel embarrassed by the way we played. We did it well below our standard, and we feel that we have to compensate our followers in some way. It's a gesture to their great loyalty," explained Melchiot. Each ticket had cost about $25, so the Wigan squad raised $10,000 for their grateful fans.

Arsenal FC's officials had a similar attitude in August 2011 after their squad was destroyed by Manchester United FC at Old Trafford, 8 to 2. Almost 3,000 fans of the London team were "compensated" with a free ticket for the next match away from home. A consolation for having traveled 435 miles, round trip, to witness the worst defeat in 115 years, since the red-shirt club fell 8-0 to Loughborough AFC on December 12, 1896, in the English second division.

In Italy, the punishment that fell on the players of Juventus FC, La Vecchia Signora, was very heavy. On May 30, 1993, by round 33 of Serie A, the powerful Turin squad was beaten mercilessly, 5-1, during its visit to the Adriatic stadium of the modest club Pescara Calcio, which had been relegated several rounds before and that season finished in the last place of the standings. The embarrassment was not free for stars like the Englishman David Platt, the Germans Jürgen Kohler and Andreas Möller, the Brazilian Júlio César, or the Italians Gianluca Vialli, Roberto Baggio or Fabrizio Ravanelli: Each one suffered a $14,000 deduction from their salary for the shameful beating.

OLYMPIC GOALS

The field was slippery and icy. Winter was felt strongly in Brockville Park, the home stadium of the Scottish club Falkirk FC, which on February 21, 1953, made Celtic FC, their rival in the third round of the Scottish Cup, feel the harshness of their surroundings. The home squad was up 2-0 in just 18 minutes and was threatening to give their Glasgow opponent a historic win. However, the green-and-white team managed to weather the storm and go to halftime without Falkirk extending their advantage. At 8 minutes into the second half, Celtic got a corner kick from the right that was taken by Northern Ireland native Charlie Tully, owner of an exquisite left-footer. Tully took two steps and launched a precise shot that placed the ball in the corner of the crossbar and the far post, with the goalkeeper Archie McFeat unable to do anything to stop it. Amazing goal, although referee Douglas Gerrard invalidated it because, in his opinion, Tully had placed the ball outside the quarter circle painted in the corner spot. Without flinching or rehearsing any protest, the Celtic kicker returned to kick the ball, this time clearly within the corresponding area, and executed a twin shot of the previous one that, again, entered the upper right corner despite McFeat's attempts to stop it. The magnificent "double play" warmed Celtic's frozen men, who at 59 minutes tied with a goal by Willie Fernie and got the victory seven minutes later with a goal by Jimmy McGrory.

In the 1991/92 Argentine Primera B tournament, Club Atlético San Miguel forward Jorge Almirón scored two Olympic goals against CA Ituzaingó goalkeeper Miguel Ángel Serrato. In this case, the two goals were validated, and San Miguel won 2 to 1.

During the 1979 edition of the Copa Libertadores, Asociación Deportivo Cali de Colombia beat Quilmes AC of Argentina 3-2, with two Olympic goals scored by Ángel Torres and Ernesto Álvarez.

In January 1991, midfielder Paul Comstive of Bolton Wanderers FC scored three goals for AFC Bournemouth, two of which were the product of corner kicks.

Bernd Nickel, legendary player of Eintracht Frankfurt of Germany, was an efficient performer of corner shots. Throughout his career, he achieved Olympic goals from the four corners of the "Eagles" stadium, Commerzbank-Arena, popularly known as Waldstadion. His victims were FC Bayern München (November 22, 1975), Fußball-Club Kaiserslautern (April 19, 1980), Sport-Verein Werder von 1899 E.V. Bremen (November 14, 1981), and Düsseldorfer Turn-und Sportverein Fortuna 1895 (May 15, 1982).

It is said that the late Turkish striker Sükrü Gülesin scored 32 Olympic goals in his prolific career for clubs Besiktas J.K., Galatasaray S.K., USC Palermo, and S.S. Lazio.

In March 2004, Mark Pulling, player of Worthing FC—a club that participates in the Isthmian League, a semi-professional tournament in the southwest region of England—beat Corinthian-Casuals FC with three goals from the same corner spot. Of course, Pulling, in addition to an excellent strike, had the help of a strong and constant wind to reach this unusual hat trick.

A THING OF BEAUTY

With the right leg, with the left, with the head, with the chest, with the hand (if the referee and his assistants don't notice the little trick). With the ball in motion, free kick, penalty. From inside the area or from outside. In favor or against. There are ways and ways to reach the goal, defined as "the orgasm of soccer" by the Uruguayan writer Eduardo Galeano. Although, of course, some are extravagant, like the one that occurred in the 1962 Paulista Championship, when Santos FC received Guarani FC at the Urbano Caldeira stadium in Santos (also known as Vila Belmiro, the name of the neighborhood in which it is located). Pelé, number "10" for the hosts, received the ball inside the box, picked it up, and made three consecutive maneuvers over the heads of three astonished defenders. After overcoming the last defender, and without allowing the ball to touch the ground, "O Rei" shot with his right leg; the ball hit the crossbar, bounced on the ground, and went far from the net. A player from Guarani pressed on, eager to continue the play, but referee João Etzel pointed to the center of the field. "The entire Guarani team went after him to claim that the ball had not crossed the line," Pelé said years later. "To end the argument, the referee shouted: 'Although it did not go in, I authorize the goal because the play was very beautiful. It was Pelé's goal, and that's all there is to it.' If I had not heard it myself, I would not have believed it."

EJECTION ON WHEELS

Ninety minutes had passed, and Ghana, the home team, was losing the 2008 CAF Africa Cup of Nations semifinal against Cameroon in the bustling Ohene Djan Sports stadium in Accra. That February 7, 2008, the Indomitable Lions defended tooth and nail a major victory sustained by a goal by Alain Nkong at 71 minutes. In the beginning of the brief period of added time, the defender Rigobert Song from the away team was lying on the grass after colliding with his own goalkeeper, Idriss Kameni, and the attacking opponent, Junior Agogo. Immediately, a cart with Ghanaian auxiliaries entered the field to remove the Cameroonian captain and allow the game to resume quickly. But, between the auxiliaries and Song was interposed, furious, another of the visitors' defenders, Andre Bikey-Amougou, who began shoving the intruders, one of which ended up buried headfirst in the grass. The Moroccan referee, Abderrahim El-Arjoun, was strict in applying the rules and dismissed the Cameroonian defender. Cameroon clinched their victory and qualified for the final, although there, without the vital presence of suspended Bikey-Amougou, they fell 1-0 to Egypt.

A RED CARD HAT TRICK

Dundee FC's 2-1 defeat during their visit to Clyde FC on December 16, 2006, for the Scottish Football League First Division, Scotland's second tier, made the striker Andy McLaren very nervous. Although there was still time to equalize the score—there were two minutes left and at least three more for injury time—McLaren forgot about the opposing goal and landed a blow to his rival Eddie Malone. The cunning action was noticed by the referee, Dougie McDonald, who extracted his red card to throw off the visiting player. But McLaren, a man who, besides his violent temper, had already had problems with drugs and alcohol, was not to be deterred. Before crossing Broadwood Stadium's sideline, he slammed his fist into the face of Clyde defender Michael McGowan. While the boxer was taken away by his own teammates and some assistants, McDonald approached and again showed the red card to the player who had already been expelled. But the incident did not end there. After the game, and with the score unchanged, McLaren ran to the referee's dressing room to try to save his career. But, finding the door closed and McDonald refusing to talk, the forward hurled a violent kick that broke through the door of the dressing room. The referee went out to the passageway and showed his red card to McLaren for the third time that same afternoon. Of course, McDonald, who was not stupid, displayed his unnecessary gesture while the furious Andy was held by a dozen policemen. Four days later, McLaren suffered a severe setback: The Court suspended him for eight matches, and his own club cut off his contract. The managers did not forgive him for being the only player in history who received three red cards in a single match, thus tainting Dundee FC's name.

THROWN OUT FOR BEING A GOAL WRECKER

In 1975, Athlone Town FC hosted Saint Patrick Athletic FC in Saint Mel's Park for the Irish League first division. Bored by the remarkable dominance of his team, the goalkeeper for the host team, Mick O'Brien, began to hang on the crossbar until he managed to sit on top of it. But the wood, somewhat worn, could not bear O'Brien's weight and broke. The goalkeeper was lying on top of the net of the destroyed goal when the referee, who had already observed the reproachful behavior of O'Brien, showed him the red card. The match continued after a local carpenter fixed the broken crossbar.

FAST REDS

Dozens of players around the world have been shown the red card without touching the ball for insulting or attacking an opponent before entering the game. In first division matches, the fastest was the Brazilian Zé Carlos of Cruzeiro Esporte Clube, who was sent off 7 seconds after the start of the Minas Gerais derby against Clube Atlético Mineiro for a violent foul. On the afternoon of July 12, 2009, when the whistle blew at the Mineirão stadium, Zé Carlos crossed the midline and elbowed Renan, one of his rivals. The referee, Paulo Cesar Oliveira, showed him the red without hesitation. With a man up for the whole match, Atlético Mineiro prevailed 0-3 and climbed thus to the top of the "Brasileirão." The Cruzeiro striker crushed the record established by Guiseppe Lorenzo from Bologna FC 1909, who had seen the red card at 10 seconds of their match against Parma FC on December 9, 1990.

The record in professional soccer, although in a lower level, occurred on December 28, 2008, in the English Southern Premier Division. That day, in the match between Chippenham Town FC and Bashley FC, host striker David Pratt shot off to the opposite field as soon as the match started and tackled the away team's midfielder Chris Knowles. The referee Justin Amey immediately took out his red card and left Chippenham Town with one man less at 3 seconds of the match. Bashley took advantage and won 1-2.

Can a red card be given any sooner? Of course, though this would be one of the most bizarre situations in the history of soccer. On October 8, 2000, to start the Taunton East Reach Wanderers–Cross Farm Celtic clash for the third division of the Sunday League of Taunton in the south of England, the referee Pete Kearle blew his whistle hard without noticing that he was barely inches from the ear of one of the players, the away team's striker Lee Todd. The boy, who was waiting with his back to the ref for the start of the match, jumped, surprised by the shrill whistle. "Fuck, shit, that's strong!" he shouted. The referee assumed that the 22-year-old had insulted him and with a quick gesture drew out his red card. The referee acted so quickly that the scene, although it seems more extensive here, unfolded in only two seconds! It was no use that Todd swore by his ancestors that he wasn't insulting the ref but was expressing surprise after being startled by the blast, Kearle did not want to reverse his decision. Todd left the field, and a few days later suffered a new setback when the Football Association suspended him for 35 days and applied a fine of 27 pounds. Among such misfortune, the striker was left with the consolation that his team, with a man less for the whole game, won a sensational 11-2 victory.

EXPELLED AFTER PLAYING

The Venetian Mattia Collauto, with a vast career of almost 500 matches in the Italian B and C divisions, will never forget the ill-fated afternoon of March 7, 1999, at the Giovanni Zini stadium. The midfielder of US Cremonese, who had been substituted after 66 minutes, chose to continue watching the match that his club was winning 1-0 from the substitute bench. In the second minute of added time, Treviso FC equaled the contest after a controversial play. Irritated to know that there had been a foul from one of the away team's players prior to the goal that tied the score, Collauto returned to the field to discuss the matter with the referee. Well, not really to discuss things, but rather to directly insult the referee. The Venetian, in this way, received a red card 26 minutes after being taken off the field!

FORGIVENESS IN BLOCK LETTERS

The players for the Swiss team Fussballclub Sankt Gallen 1879 came out red-faced with shame of the Sportpark Bergholz stadium. The 11-3 defeat at Fussball Club Wil 1900, which occurred on November 3, 2002, had hit the humiliated players hard. To apologize for the embarrassment—especially since it was the Sankt Gallen canton derby against their "younger brother"—the players and their coach, Thomas Staub, decided to buy a whole page of the local newspaper St. Gallen TagBlatt to express their condolences to the distressed fans. "We, the players of FC St. Gallen, made a fool of ourselves," read the heading in block letters, accompanied by a photograph of the team and the signature of each player. "We know that you are the best fans in Switzerland, and we have disappointed you. We are very sorry, unfortunately, we cannot turn back the clock," added the remorseful gentlemen. Anyway, the apology should not have been very expensive, since the St. Gallen TagBlatt newspaper was the main sponsor of the team...

THE SURPRISE

Anxiety enveloped Tom O'Kane as he sat in his seat on the train. The impatient defender felt that, on that evening of September 12, 1885, the convoy traveled the 15 miles that separate the cities of Dundee and Arbroath extremely slowly. O'Kane, fullback for Dundee Harp FC, could not wait to return to his village to strut in front of his former teammates of Arbroath FC—with whom he had ended up quarreling to the death—for the tremendous beating his team had just given Aberdeen Rovers FC in the first round of the Scottish Cup: 35-0. O'Kane, who had dared to send a telegram to Gayfield Park to humiliate his former comrades, also planned to brag that the score had been even wider: the referee had validated 37 goals, but a manager of the same Harp, perhaps more pious than their modest rivals in the north, had warned the man in black that he was wrong, probably because of the absence of nets in the goals, which would be patented five years later, and that it had "only" been 35. Thus, the number, the most gigantic in the incipient history of British soccer, was officially sealed. As soon as he got off the train, O'Kane ran to the Arbroath FC stadium, where his former team had just faced, also for the National Cup, Bon Accord FC, coincidentally another Aberdeen team. The defender almost fainted: His former comrades had destroyed their rivals by 36 to 0! Amused by the strange situation and the face of O'Kane, the boys from Arbroath added to the surprise: They complained that the referee, Dave Stormont, had invalidated seven goals for offside, with which the score would have been 43-0. They also told him that not only had their goalkeeper, Jim Milne, not touched the ball the whole match, but he had also followed the play of the uneven game under an umbrella handed to him by a spectator to protect himself from the copious rain that had given no respite during the 90 minutes.

The remarkable victory of Arbroath—which remains the largest in the history of British soccer—is probably explained by the fact that the Scottish federation made a mistake when it formulated its invitations to the tournament. Instead of summoning Aberdeeen's Orion FC, the letter was forwarded by mistake to Orion Cricket Club, an institution in that same city where soccer was not practiced. However, the cricket players accepted the treat and signed up as "Bon Accord," an expression that emerged during the Scottish independence wars, to differentiate themselves, precisely, from the other Orion club.

More incredible data from that day consists of the results of many of the other 47 matches that took place: Alpha FC, 6, Cambuslang Hibernian FC, 8; Ayr FC, 7, Maybole FC, 0; Ayr Rovers FC, 0, Dalry FC, 8; Coupar Angus FC, 2, Dundee Our Boys FC, 8; Crieff FC, 0, Dunfermline Athletic FC, 7; Granton FC, 0, Partick Thistle FC, 11; Greenock Southern FC, 1, Neilston FC, 10; Hibernian FC, 9, Edina Hibs FC, 0; Kilmarnock FC, 7, Annbank United FC, 1; Kirkintilloch Athletic, 0, Renton FC, 15; Queen's Park FC, 16, St. Peter's FC, 0; Shettleston FC, 1, Cambuslang FC, 7; Strathmore FC, 7, Aberdeen FC, 0; Third Lanark A.C., 9, Shawlands FC, 1; Thistle FC, 11, Westbourne FC, 1; Vale of Teith FC, 9, Oban FC, 1—these are just some of those, that, more than a hundred years later, seem exaggerated.

Finally, an additional rarity: Just as with other clubs or teams with great winning scores mentioned in this chapter, neither Arbroath FC nor Dundee Harp FC managed to reach even the round of 16; the former beat Forfar Athletic FC 9-1 in the second round, in third they beat Dundee East End FC 7-1, and in the fourth (round of 16) fell to Hibernian FC 5-3; the latter defeated successively Dundee Our Boys FC 4-1 and Vale of Teith FC 8-1, then were crushed by Vale of Leven FAC 6-0.

COMPASSION

On February 28, 1980, the stands of the World Cup stadium in the city of Mendoza empty, CA Huracán, having one of the best teams in the first division of Argentina, destroyed the local semiprofessional team Gutiérrez Fútbol Club 12 to 0 in the final of the Vintage Cup. Dante Adrián Sanabria (at 4 and 34 minutes), Miguel Brindisi (18'), Roque Avallay (19'), René Houseman (33', 35', 41', and 46'), Carlos Babington (45', penalty kick), and Juan César Silva (58', 60', and 73') established at the net the abysmal difference of quality between the two teams. When the "Hot Air Balloon" team scored its twelfth goal, an employee of the Malvinas Argentinas stadium, a Gutiérrez fan, wrote in the giant electronic board of the stadium: "Enough with the goals please!" The unusual request softened the boys of Huracán who, after reading the appeal, took pity on their weak rival and didn't return to their penalty box in the remaining 17 minutes.

PRIORITIES

The directors and players of the Finland national team were fascinated by the possibility of getting to know Paris, to such an extent that the game corresponding to the qualifying stage for the 1962 World Cup in Chile was perceived more as a holiday than as a hard soccer match. The Finns, who had already lost at home 1-2 against the French squad and 0-2 against Bulgaria and were practically eliminated, took advantage of their first time in the City of Lights to visit the most attractive spots in the French capital, such as the Eiffel Tower and the Arc de Triomphe, and attend a cabaret show at the famous "Casino de Paris"...the night before the match. They cared so little about the match that they did not even rent a field for a final workout. On September 28, 1961, at the Parc des Princes, the effect of champagne and bohemian life undermined the legs of the northerners so much so that France imposed itself effortlessly by winning 5 to 1.

THE SOUVENIR

Founded in 1880, Selkirk Football Club is one of the oldest teams in Scotland, although it always played in amateur tournaments, such as the East of Scotland Football League. In 1984, the players of this club from the small town of Selkirk decided to register in the prestigious Scottish Cup. The draw of the first phase determined that their first rival would be Stirling Albion, a professional team, although at that time sailing in the second division. Even in the first round, the Selkirk boys decided to face the match as if it were a final and got together several days in advance to plan strategy. On the morning of December 8, the amateur team traveled almost 60 miles to present themselves, with great expectation, at the Doubletree Dunblane Stadium in Stirling. Sadly, their hope dissipated in a few minutes. The first half ended 15-0 for the home squad, who scored with eight different players. The inexperienced away players improved a bit in the second half and only allowed the hosts to score another five goals. In spite of such bad luck, the Selkirk goalkeeper, Richard Taylor, left with a smile: His rivals had given him the ball of the match as a souvenir.

SOCCER WAKES

Many fans have had their funeral services held on soccer fields, but only one while playing a first division game. On March 27, 2011, during the second half of the confrontation between Cúcuta Deportivo FC and Envigado FC at the General Santander stadium for the eighth round of the tournament in Colombia, several members of the *Banda del Indio* (the Native's Firm), the *"barra brava"* of Cúcuta, evaded the police security controls and entered the stands carrying a coffin wrapped with a red and black cloth, inside which was the body of a teenager. "Alex is not dead; he's still alive inside," sang about 200 fans. Cristopher Alexander Jácome Sanguino, 17, had been shot dead a week earlier during a soccer brawl. The kid was shot four times when he participated in a 5-a-side soccer match in the Bellavista neighborhood. The members of the *Banda del Indio* were forbidden to enter the stadium for having staged numerous acts of violence. However, during the second half, the hooligans took advantage of an open gate and went through carrying with the coffin on their backs. The president of the Corporación Nuevo Cúcuta Deportivo, Álvaro Torrado Sagra, took the blame off him for the incident and instead blamed the National Police for being "responsible for the safety of the spectacle." The boy's mother, when interviewed by the local newspaper *El Tiempo*, said that she authorized the unusual wake because "he wanted that, exactly, to be his farewell." When the referee marked the end of the game (1-1), the funeral cortege moved the coffin to the house of the boy's family to be buried the next day.

A similar episode occurred in October 2012 at the stadium of the Argentine team Quilmes AC, although during a reserves match against CA Unión of Santa Fe, which was taking place without an audience. In this case, the coffin belonged to a young man who had died during a gun fight, apparently between two rival gangs. The boy, moreover, was the son of one of the leaders of the Quilmes *"barra brava."* The funeral procession took place in one of the stands at 10 minutes during the second half of the match. Unión goalkeeper, Joaquin Papaleo, ran to the middle of the field, visibly scared. Later, in his account of the event on Twitter, he would assure everyone that the intruders "shot a couple of bullet shots" while paying homage to the deceased boy. The game was interrupted and only resumed when the procession left the stadium. Senator Anibal Fernandez, president of Quilmes and former chief of staff of then President Cristina de Kirchner, said during a radio interview: "I do not see that anything bad has been done."

INOPPORTUNE JUDGMENT

The small Tuscan stadium Alberto Benedetti simmered that afternoon of March 7, 2010. Unione Sportiva Borgo a Buggiano 1920 was tied at 0 goals with the visitors, Football Club Fossombrone from the neighboring province of Pesaro and Urbino, and their possibilities of winning the regional zone of the Campionato Nazionale Dilettanti, the Italian "Serie D," were weakening. At 15 minutes into the second half, referee Andrea Bonavia called a controversial penalty and expelled the home team's goalkeeper Matteo Cherubini. Fossombrone's captain, the midfielder Francesco Marianeschi, beat substitute goalkeeper Matteo Costa with a portentous shot, and in the stands the blue fans exploded, insulting the referee, who they blamed for the partial defeat. One of the most excited was Roberto Luporini, director of Borgo a Buggiano, who, in the middle of the protest, suffered a heart attack and died shortly after at the edge of the field. The tragic news shot quickly to the pitch, where the aggrieved host players begged Bonavia to stop play. The ref consulted the rival "captain," Marianeschi, and with his consent suspended the match at 71 minutes. However, in assessing what happened, the Competition Committee issued a disconcerting ruling three days later: They gave the match as lost to the home squad, penalized them by taking away another point, and fined them 1,000 euros for understanding that their players had left the field without a valid reason. The committee did not consider the death of Luporini as a "force majeure" reason that justified the suspension of the match and punished the Tuscan team as they saw fit. The board of Borgo a Buggiano did not sit idly by and appeared before the Federal Court of Justice, in Rome, to complain about what they considered an unjust punishment.

After analyzing everything that happened, the high court dismissed the resolution of the committee and ordered the game to resume. On April 28, the Fossombrone Football Club boys went back the 120 miles to return to the Alberto Benedetti and completed the remaining 19 minutes with their colleagues Bordo Buggiano and a new referee, Fabio Ghellere. With ten players, the hosts couldn't turn the score around, but, at least they had pleasure of paying tribute to their beloved Luporini in the playing field.

OMERTÀ

Befor the game with Strongoli Calico began, Pasqualino Arena, president of the club ASD Isola Capo Rizzuto 1966, approached the young referee, Paolo Zimmaro, and with tears in his eyes begged him to observe a minute of silence to remember his cousin, Carmine Arena, who had died a few days before and was a fanatic "tifoso" of the squad. Zimmaro felt sorry for the executive and, with the two teams lined up in their respective sides, he whistled for the start of the tribute on October 4, 2004, during the pre-match for Group A of the Promozione championship in the Calabria region. Of course, the naive referee—an inexperienced 20-year-old engineering student—did not know that the deceased had not been a simple and innocent fan in life, but a "capo" of the 'Ndrangheta, the powerful Calabrian mafia. He had been killed by being shot three times with a bazooka and from several blasts of Kalashnikov automatic rifles while driving his armored car! The incident quickly came to the attention of Crotone prosecutor Franco Tricoli, who, while repudiating the distinction of a mafioso during a sporting event, acknowledged that the referee had been misled. "They made the request to me just when we were going down to the field; they told me that a person close to the club had died and only at the end of the game did I learn the truth," Zimmaro admitted before the regional referees committee. The young man was not prosecuted by Tricoli but suspended along with his assistant referees for allowing the homage without authorization.

PUNISHED REVERENCE

Argentino del Sud and CA Almagro had to face each other on June 30, 1929, for the last round of the first division tournament of the Asociación Amateur Argentina de Football. However, when they arrived at the stadium of Argentino, in the town of Sarandí, the members of both teams learned that the day before Adrián Beccar Varela, the president of the club, had died (five years later it would be renamed Asociación del Fútbol Argentino, its current name). As a tribute to the deceased leader, in view of the fact that the match wasn't very important for the two squads—they did not fight for the title and both had already been saved from relegation—the players agreed to suspend the match as a sign of mourning. Incredibly, the laudable gesture was harshly questioned by the Amateur Association of Argentinian Football! In an extremely severe ruling, the institution decided to cancel the match between the two clubs for having decided to suspend the match without consulting the institution. The teams did not protest, instead opting for a pious minute of silence.

THE UNNECESSARY RED

In the mid-1990s, an amazing case occurred in the Spanish city of Salamanca. While two combined teams of under-16 players faced each other, a dog that wanted to join in the fun crossed the line of chalk to run behind the ball. The uninvited player was stopped by the referee, who whistled to the dog and showed him the red card. The dog surprised everyone with his apparent knowledge of the rules of the game. When he saw the red card, he turned around, and, without even a parting bark, withdrew from the pitch over the end line.

UNINVITED GUESTS

For the Romanian players, the defeat against Israel (0-1, March 18, 1998) had an extremely "rational" explanation. The field chosen by the federation for that friendly in preparation for the 1998 World Cup in France, Stadionul Steaua, was cursed. "Here, you can sense the gloomy atmosphere," the players assured their coach, Anghel Iordănescu. Several of them thought they saw ghosts running around the field. The players attributed the grim situation to the fact that Stadionul Steaua was next to a cemetery and said that they did not want to return to that place, fearing that the power of the specters would conjure up a spell that would make them fail in the Cup. The directors and the managerial staff, as superstitious as the players, agreed and looked for another training ground for the next practice match against Greece on April 8: Arena Națională. There, without terrifying spirits circling the field, Romania won the game 2-1, and, in France, the Eastern European squad finished first and undefeated in their group stage ahead of England, Colombia, and Tunisia.

THE SUSPENSION

The tackle made by Luiggi Coluccio, defender of L'Unione Sportiva Gioiosa Jonica, to ASD forward Bocale Calcio was vicious. The immediate red card was justified that afternoon of October 29, 1995, in which both teams faced each other for the Promozione de Calabria championship. Three days later, when Coluccio, 23, was alone closing his bar, two armed men came to his establishment and shot him dead. The crime, according to the police, was linked to an alleged settling of accounts of the 'Ndrangheta. Once again. The mafia organization had already set fire to a restaurant and a small supermarket of the same family, and Luiggi's brother, Pasquale, had received a bullet in the arm. Nine days after the crime, after analyzing the report of the referee, the federation decided to suspend the dead man for a match! The head of the regional commission, Nino Cosentino, explained that "the disciplinary mechanism is inflexible" and "had already been launched" with the report that the referee had completed before the homicide. To repudiate the bloody murder, in their next game, U.S. Gioiosa Jonica faced A.S. Sambatello Calcio wearing black bracelets. And, to fulfill the ridiculous verdict, they left the number "2" jersey in the locker room. Coluccio's substitute wore the "14." Gioiosa Jonica won 1-0 thanks to a goal scored in the last minute. And the men celebrated by looking toward the sky.

THE ENEMY AT HOME

There is no team that doesn't complain about the performance of the referees. What is strange is that a national team would rant against a referee who had not even officiated for them and, in addition, was from their own country! The particular episode occurred on July 15, 2004, during the Copa América that was played in Peru. Costa Rica and Chile were fighting for third place in Group C at the Modelo Jorge Basadre stadium in Tacna, in which Paraguay and Brazil had already gone through to the next round. The winner would also join the round of 16, as CONMEBOL regulations specified that the two best third ranked teams out of the three groups would make it to the quarterfinals. The three minutes added on by the Bolivian referee René Ortubé had already been completed, and the score was still tied 1-1. Apparently entertained by the actions, the referee allowed the men to continue for a while until Costa Rican Andy Herrón scored a goal, qualifying the Central American team and eliminating, at the same time, Chile and...Bolivia, third of the Group A! If Ortubé had finished the match at the right time, the Andean squad would have continued in the competition. When he returned home, as could be expected, the Bolivian referee was not precisely greeted by happy faces.

THE HAIL STONE OF RELEGATION

At the end of 1894, Walsall Town Swifts FC, "father" of the current Wallsall FC and one of the founders of the English second division, found itself in a difficult situation. The club urgently needed a win to escape relegation—and disaffiliation, which was the norm for those who finished at the bottom of the standings of what was, at that time, the last professional division—and on December 29, 1894, against Newcastle United FC, a victory was worth as much as gold. However, the first half was disastrous for the home team: first, because one of their men, Robert Willis, suffered an injury that forced him to leave the field; second, because with one man up, "the magpies" feasted and retired victorious 0-3 at halftime. In the second half, Walsall, with wounded pride, went on the attack, despite the numerical disadvantage, and in a few minutes managed to get back two goals, placing themselves inches away from the tie. At 78 minutes, when the draw seemed certain, a black cloud covered the sky and unleashed a strong hail. The fury of the storm forced the referee to suspend the match to protect the players. A few days later, the Football Association resolved to set the result in favor of Newcastle, a decision that was appealed by the directors of the defeated team, who considered that there were still 12 valuable minutes to play and reverse the result. However, after a second analysis, the entity ratified its decision, and at the end of the season, Walsall was the last of the three relegations despite having the same points as Lincoln City FC, which retained its place in the division, thanks to a better difference of goals in favor. A year later, this club returned to the second division, although with a new name: Walsall FC. The "Town Swifts" had been buried under a cold hailstorm.

TELL THE RAIN

It has already been seen here that, when the rain is abundant but not enough to stifle the enthusiasm for soccer, strange (and humid) situations often arise. In 1899, Brussels Racing Club and Athletic and Running Club fought for the first division tournament in Belgium in the middle of a copious downpour that kept away all but three spectators. The away team won 0-3, so you could say that the game had an average of one goal per fan!

CA Talleres de Córdoba and CA Rosario Central began their match on April 25, 1999, for the ninth round of the Argentine Clausura. A storm had erased the field's sidelines and end lines, which had to be repainted a short time before of the initial whistle.

On July 16, 1995, during the Copa América that was played in Uruguay, the organizers used a helicopter to dry the pitch of the Centenario stadium on which a lot of rain had fallen and two consecutive games had to be played: Colombia vs. Paraguay and Uruguay vs. Bolivia.

WELCOMED INJURY

There is nothing players hate more than injuries and blows. However, sometimes a bang can be very welcomed, Khiat Ahmed can attest. In 1961, Ahmed, 20 years old, had lost his voice when a projectile exploded next to him during a battle in the War of Liberation when Algeria fought for independence from France. Three years later, during a first division match of that nation in North Africa, Ahmed—now a soccer player—received a hit from an unseen ball that knocked him down and stunned him for several minutes. When Ahmed recovered…it was a miracle! He had recovered his speech! What were his first words, you may ask? Nothing too splendid. Just very bad insults at the referee for an alleged wrong call against his team...

BLOW

"If you score again, it'll be the last goal of your life," warned Altrincham FC's fierce defender bitterly. An ultimatum that was a bit too cruel for a game of the English youth in 1924. However, William "Dixie" Dean, the player from Tranmere Rovers FC with the most promise, was not intimidated and, a few minutes later, returned to send the ball to the back of the net. It was his last time touching the ball. During the next play, the wild defender fulfilled his threat and mercilessly kicked Dean in the groin. Dean fell down, overcome with pain. The boy was hospitalized immediately and had to face the removal of a testicle which had burst upon being kicked. But Dean recovered and, instead of cowering, unleashed a huge career with 447 league matches and 390 goals, plus 18 goals in 16 games with England. Dean is still the owner of the record of goals in a single season of English soccer. With the Everton FC jersey, he scored 60 goals in the 1927/28 championship.

THEY MAY BREAK BUT THEY WON'T STOP

Until 1970, when FIFA authorized players' substitutions, many were forced to remain on the field so that they didn't leave their team with inferior numbers, even when they had suffered terrible injuries. Some emblematic cases happened during the most important tournament, the World Cup. In the quarterfinals of France 1938, the Czech goalkeeper Frantisek Planicka remained firm under the posts when his team went up against Brazil, even though he had suffered a fracture. Some versions claim that the radius of one of his arms had been broken; others, a clavicle. The goalkeeper stoically endured the second half and the extra time, which ended in a draw. Two days later, in the rematch, Planicka was replaced by Karel Burket.

In one of the semifinals of Switzerland 1954, the Uruguayan Juan Hohberg refused to leave the field against Hungary despite having suffered a heart attack, and in Chile 1962, another Uruguayan, Eliseo Álvarez, kept running after the ball after fracturing the fibula of his left leg.

These extreme measures can be justified by the level of the competition and the rule against substitutions. Perhaps that's why it's hard to understand why the Portuguese midfielder for the Spanish team Valencia CF, Manuel Fernandes, played 75 minutes with a broken fibula. Fernandes hurt himself 15 minutes after the clash with Getafe CF had started on Sunday, April 5, 2009.

Despite having noticed a pain in his left ankle, the Lusitanian midfielder was able to finish the match by keeping the tibia (the thickest bone of the calf) immobile with the medical bandage used by soccer players. When the Valencian club's doctor, Antonio Giner, diagnosed the fracture, Fernandes underwent surgery and missed the rest of the season.

In 1999, the goalkeeper for Club Nacional Fútbol of Uruguay, Gustavo Munúa, played all of the superclásico against CA Peñarol for the Mercosur Cup with a fracture in the left forearm. Munúa had been injured several days earlier during a local league match against Club Deportivo Maldonado when he collided with an opponent. The morning after that match, the goalie noticed his arm felt uncomfortable, but the Nacional doctor only prescribed ice to reduce inflammation in the damaged limb. After the duel with Peñarol, the goalkeeper discovered that the swelling had worsened, so he resorted to another specialist, a traumatic injuries expert. This expert immediately noticed the problem and that same day operated on the goalkeeper of the Uruguayan national team which was runner-up in the Malaysian World Youth Championship 1997.

A month after Munúa's adventures, Claudio Arzeno, Argentine defender of Real Racing Club of Santander of Spain, scored a goal with his face in front of Reial Club Deportiu Espanyol of Barcelona. The impact with the ball not only knocked down the former Independiente defender, but also fractured his nose. After being assisted by the doctor of the Cantabrian squad, Arzeno recovered and continued to play the remaining 65 minutes of the match. "I did not think about leaving the field; I thought it was nothing because I could breathe through my mouth," the central defender explained at the end of the match, which tied at two goals.

In one of the matches of the great campaign of 1960, which allowed his team, CA Los Andes, to achieve promotion to the first division of Argentina, the goalkeeper Leon Goldbaum was hit by a player of the opposing team. The blow fractured three ribs, putting him in a cast. But nothing could stop Goldbaum. The following Saturday, he put the number "1" jersey over his hard shell and went out with his teammates.

Continuing with goalies: In August 2009, the Argentine goalkeeper of the Club Deportivo Cali Association, Sebastián Blázquez, was diagnosed with a broken fibula...two weeks after the injury occurred! To top it all, in that period, Blázquez played in two games, convinced that it was only a muscle strain. "At no time did I imagine that I had played two games with such an injury," the goalkeeper acknowledged. The fracture occurred on August 18 in a training session prior to a match against Club Universidad de Chile for the Copa Sudamericana. "They hit me in the left fibula, halfway up the leg; it was like a joke from a partner who wanted to make me lose stability. I thought it was just a blow. I never thought I had a broken bone. I injected painkillers (to play against Universidad de Chile), but I ended up with a lot of pain. During the week I improved a little, and the next Sunday (August 23) I faced Quindío. In the first half I had no problems, but after 15 minutes of the second I started to feel pain and asked to leave." The following week, the goalkeeper said, "We continued with the recovery. I tried to work. Thursday came, and it didn't improve enough to play against Tolima (August 30), and I was given rest. We thought that without demanding much of the muscle it could improve. In the first days of October, as the discomfort persisted, we did an MRI and it came out that I had a fracture, a broken bone from end to end." An incredible record.

BREAKING POINT

An unusual episode was set against the French team Association Sportive Nancy-Lorraine in mid-1971 during a first division match. In the first half, two defenders, Jean Pierre Borgoni and René Woltrager, collided with each other and broke the right leg and hip, respectively. The unfortunate day continued in the second half when the goalie Jean Paul Krafft fractured his skull after colliding with another teammate, Eddy Dublin.

Bobby Blackwood, defender for the English team Colchester United FC, broke his jaw in August 1966 after colliding with Les Allen, forward for Queen's Park Rangers FC in a game of the Third Division. After a four-month recovery, Blackwood returned to the field, coincidentally, against QPR. The defender again fractured his jaw in a new collision with Les Allen!

The victory that CA River Plate won by 3 to 1 against their archrival CA Boca Juniors on November 19, 1933, had a very special flavor, because the *millionaires* had to play with one man down for 80 minutes, since at that time substitutions were not allowed. In the 10th minute, defender Roberto Basílico broke his arm after colliding with *xeneize* striker Francisco Varallo. This accident was very curious since the defender, in the previous *Superclásico* played on July 2, had broken his clavicle after being pounced on by Varallo!

The French referee Patrick Lhermite is a good example of the fact that referees are not exempt from complications. On April 20, 2003, during a match of "Le Championnat" between the Jeunesse Auxerroise Association and Le Havre Athletic Club Football Association, Lhermite was accidentally run over by a player and suffered a double fracture of the tibia and fibula. The ref had to be removed on a stretcher and replaced by the fourth referee, Jean Marc Rodolphe, who completed the remaining half hour of play.

In this sense, what happened to Eli Cohen, coach of the Israeli club Hapoel Akko AFC, is even more surprising. On September 21, 2011, while playing the first half of a match between his team and Hapoel Tel Aviv FC for the first division of the Middle East nation, one of Akko's defenders, Roei Levi, stopped a rival advance with a violent clearing toward the stands. Well, not exactly, because the ball, instead of falling in the stands, hit Cohen's arm, who was standing behind the sideline and only a foot away from the impulsive Levi. The blow fractured a few bones in Cohen's hand, who in no way was daunted by the mishap. For the second half, he returned to the bench with a bulky bandage. What the press did not broadcast is what the coach said to his player during halftime.

CURSED CURRY

Levi Foster, midfielder for the English amateur club AFC GOP, saw that referee Bunny Reid had crouched at his side to tie his shoelaces. Mischievously, Foster turned a few degrees and, when his butt was at the same height as the head of the referee, let loose a loud and stinky fart. Reid sat up, furious. Although the player attempted an absurd apology, "Sorry, I had curry last night," the referee took out his yellow card and cautioned the daring midfielder. Foster was later suspended by the disciplinary court for two rounds for the "disrespectful attitude" toward the ref. If his fault merited such a severe sanction, why didn't Reid expel him? The regulation establishes that a soccer player who incurs a sanction of "unsportsmanlike conduct" may be reprimanded or expelled. The punishment must be interpreted by the referee, a rule so volatile that, throughout the history of the sport, it has generated countless unusual "yellow" situations, as curious as the story, which happened in the city of Portsmouth in November 2009.

A CATHOLIC GESTURE

In March 1996, seconds from the start of the game between Rangers and Partick Thistle, valid for Scotland's top flight, visiting striker Rod McDonald, a Catholic, crossed himself. The attacker made the sign of the cross a little out of religious conviction and a little out of superstition, as he repeated the motion before each match. However, referee Jim McGilvray felt that his gesture had been offensive to the thousands of Protestant fans who occupied the stands of Ibrox Park and, before whistling the start of the match, approached the attacker of Partick Thistle and gave him a cautionary yellow card.

GASCOIGNE, THE JESTER

A year earlier, on the same stage—though in a clash between Rangers and Hibernian—referee Dougie Smith dropped his yellow card during the game. The card was picked up by the vivacious Paul Gascoigne, who saw the opportunity to play a small joke. The English midfielder approached Smith and, imitating the gestures of the referee, "cautioned" him with his own card, which he then returned. The joke caused a great deal of laughter in the fans, but not the referee. As soon as he received the card, he showed it to the comical Gascoigne in an attitude more typical of the law of Talion—the one that imposed as punishment "eye for an eye, tooth for tooth"—rather than that of soccer.

YELLOW MACHINE GUN

On November 3, 1969, two teams from the league of the English city of Surrey, Tongham Youth Club and Hawley, played an absolutely calm game. However, to the eyes of the referee John McAdam, the players acted with excessive violence. Throughout the match, the ref showed the yellow card to the 22 protagonists. When one of the linesmen approached him to express his disagreement, he was also warned by McAdam!

THE HONEYMOON THAT WASN'T

Chilean defender Ronald Fuentes analyzed the calendar and proposed to his girlfriend in early January 1997. Fuentes explained to his girlfriend that when the "Red" team faced Argentina in Buenos Aires for the qualifiers for the World Cup in France, he was going to be yellow-carded because, as he already had another yellow, he would receive a suspension date, and they could then leave together for their honeymoon. On December 15, 1996, when the 1-1 draw between the two teams was close to being over, Fuentes committed an intentional foul and won, as he had planned, the warning. But the clever defender did not foresee the clumsiness of the Paraguayan referee Ubaldo Aquino, who forgot to write down the punishment in the official report. As the wedding was already scheduled, Fuentes got married and went on a trip—although not with his new wife—to Lima to play the following January 12 with Peru. The situation, which was already crooked, ended up disintegrating when, a few hours before the match the Peruvian federation demanded that Fuentes comply with the restriction. The agency quickly studied the case and agreed with the request made by the local squad. Without honeymoon, without match, and without points (Chile fell by 2 to 1), the defender learned that if something can go wrong, it will.

THE TOMB

The following seems to be taken from a fantastic story about Halloween. However, it is as scary as it is true. On March 30, 1978, the Venezuelan soccer team Portuguesa Fútbol Club received Cerro Porteño from Paraguay at the José Antonio Páez stadium in the city of Acarigua to take part in a match corresponding to group 5 of the Copa Libertadores. Pedro Pascual Peralta opened the scoring for the home side, while the Paraguayan Gerardo Gonzalez got the final tying goal. Up to that point, everything was normal. In fact, the game ended without incident. However, the final whistle of the Colombian referee Orlando Sanchez gave birth to a terrible story. Sanchez and his assistants—Venezuelan Vicente Llobregat and the Peruvian Enrique Labo Revoredo—showered, changed, and got into a car heading to Caracas, where the two foreign referees planned to board the planes that would take them back to their homelands. But, about 3 miles from Acarigua, the vehicle was intercepted by a group of Portuguesa fans. The three officials were threatened with firearms and knocked out of the car. Sanchez was dragged by his hair to a field, where he was handed a shovel and forced, at gunpoint, to dig a grave where the aggressors threatened to bury his body. Terrified, the Colombian referee began to dig a hole in the ground until several police patrols appeared in time to rescue him. The Portuguesa club had to pay a fine of $5,000, and its stadium was suspended for a year. Sanchez never returned to Venezuela.

THE ICEBERG

Many soccer matches have been canceled due to heavy rain. Several by hail, fog, or snow. Some by strong winds, whirlwinds, and hurricanes. What happened on August 29, 2005, is a unique, extraordinary case in the 150 years of soccer history. A match was suspended for...the presence of an iceberg! Yes, you read that right: a gigantic iceberg! The incredible event has an explanation, of course, but framed within a complex context.

That day, one of the semifinals of the Greenland Cup was played between FC Malamuk from the city of Uummannaq and Nagdlunguaq-48 from Nuuk, the capital of Greenland. Almost completely covered with ice all year long, the island of Greenland does not have too many places to set up a sports field, and the only place that soccer fans found in Uummannaq is a rocky field lacking in turf located on the icy Baffin Bay. To access the field, which is surrounded by the sea and high, steep cliffs, players, referees, and spectators must use boats, which dock at a wharf mounted a few feet from the field of play, parallel to one of the sidelines. That day, while the men from Malamuk and Nagdlunguaq-48 were fighting for the ball, one of the almost a thousand fans who gathered to enjoy the peculiar match warned that a large iceberg—although only one-eighth of its volume— was dangerously approaching the small port and threatening to destroy the hundreds of ships moored there. The sympathizer raised the alarm, and everyone—the referee, the linesmen, and the players included—left the ball to run toward the boats, set sail, and avoid a collision. Some time later, when the iceberg had passed—though not without leaving a trail of "cubes" for whiskey next to the sidelines—and the danger gone, the game resumed and culminated with a visitor victory, 1-3.

THE WITCH

On July 26, 1981, 60,000 people filled the Nemesio Camacho stadium in Bogota to capacity to witness Colombia's debut against Peru in the qualifying round for the 1982 World Cup in Spain. For that match, the Argentine coach Carlos Bilardo, coach of the *cafeteros* ("coffee growers"), had hired a "witch" named Beatriz Becerra, a woman from Cali who was credited with supernatural powers, and took her to the stadium to help him coach. Bilardo brought the woman into the locker room to transfer her alleged gifts to the players and help the host team win. His tactics seemed to work when Pedro Zape, at 40 minutes in, stopped a penalty kick by Teófilo Cubillas. The magic continued 20 minutes into the second half when Hernán Darío Herrera opened the scoring for Colombia. But, four minutes from the end, Guillermo la Rosa scored the definitive draw. The goal deprived Colombia of starting their campaign with a victory and the witch Becerra from keeping her job: Bilardo fired her as soon as she returned to the dressing room.

A HOT CELEBRATION

Shortly before traveling to the United States to lead his team through the 2015 CONCACAF Gold Cup, Mexican national team coach Miguel "Piojo" Herrera had a fierce dispute with a journalist from Televisión Azteca, Christian Martinoli. Irritated by Martinoli's criticism of the his team's performance in the Copa América of Chile, eliminated in the first round, Herrera went out of his way during an interview with a sports channel to insult Martinoli: "There is an asshole that attacks me. One day we'll cross paths, and then I'll discuss it with him; it'll just be a debate." Martinoli, renowned for his sharp and spicy style, did not miss the criticism and responded through his Twitter account: "I love the elegance of the national coach; he's not a cheerleader, he's a barra brava." "I'm not that, but hopefully somewhere I can find you to fix the differences," Herrera insisted. Tension began to rise.

After the heated fourth and semifinal matches against Costa Rica and Panama in the 2015 Gold Cup, Mexico beat Jamaica without much effort in the final played at Lincoln Financial Field in Philadelphia, 3 to 1. The next morning, the Mexican squad arrived at the Philadelphia International Airport to board a flight back to their country. When entering the exit hall of the air station, Herrera discovered Martinoli, who had traveled to the United States to call the games on TV and who was also about to return to Mexico. Without saying a word, Herrera ran like a bull drawn to a red cape and threw a punch, hitting the journalist in the neck.

Only the intervention of another special envoy of *TV Azteca*, Luis García, prevented Herrera from injuring Martinoli even more, although at the cost of receiving some blows himself. "I'm not one to get heated like that. I was wrong. It's not what anyone should do. Things don't have to be fixed like that. I have a short fuse, yes, explosive at times, but I'm not an aggressive person," the coach defended himself hours later in another television interview. "It was a personal situation that had to do with my family, and it bothered me, and at that moment I lost my temper. I saw him, I was blinded, and that's it, but when you're a public person, you cannot make those types of decisions," he insisted.

But his statements did not help him. "Violence does not fit in society, in the family, and much less in any sport. Nobody who wants to impose themselves with aggression, and not with ideas and concepts, over the principle of freedom of expression can be a member of the Mexican Football Federation. Mexican fans deserve respect; deserve people with integrity who represent what we want our national soccer to be. Despite an extraordinary career, full of success both on the field and as a manager, the results cannot be put above our statutes, regulations, respect, and freedom of expression. The Mexican Football Federation, the different leagues that constitute it and especially those in our National Team must be an example for the new generations and what happened does not show the spirit of loyal competition that we want to promote for our national soccer," warned the president of the Mexican Football Federation, Decio de María Serrano, justifying the firing of the bellicose Herrera.

BIBLIOGRAPHY

Books

ABC - Diccionario Enciclopédico del Fútbol. 2000. AGEA, Buenos Aires.

Ash, Russell, and Morrison, Ian. 2010. *Top Ten of Football.* Hamlyn, London.

Ball, Phil. Morbo. 2003. *The Story of Spanish Football.* WSC Books Limited, London.

Barnade, Oscar. 2011. *Historias Increíbles de Argentina en la Copa América.* Ediciones Al Arco, Buenos Aires.

Barret, Norman. 2001. *The Daily Telegraph Chronicle of Football.* Carlton Books, London.

Bilardo, Carlos. 2014. *Doctor y campeón.* Editorial Planeta, Buenos Aires.

Biblioteca total del fútbol, el deporte de los cinco continentes. 1982. Editorial Océano, Madrid.

Biblioteca total del fútbol, de los orígenes al Mundial. 1982. Editorial Océano, Madrid.

Brown, Paul. 2013. *The Victorian Football Miscellany.* Superelastic, Milton Keynes.

Burns, Jimmy. 2012. *La Roja.* Nation Books, New York.

Campomar, Andreas. 2014. *Golazo.* Club House, Buenos Aires.

Carlisle, Jeff. 2009. *Soccer's Most Wanted II.* Potomac Books, Virginia.

Confederación Sudamericana de Fútbol. *Historia de la Copa América, Second Edition.*

Copa Libertadores de América - 30 años. 1990. Confederación Sudamericana de Fútbol, Buenos Aires.

Crossan, Rob. 2011. *Football Extreme.* John Blake Publishing Ltd., London.

Cruyff, Johan. 2017. *14. La autobiografía.* Editorial Planeta, Buenos Aires.

Díaz, Juan Manuel, et al. 2007. *La pelota nunca se cansa.* Editorial Base, Barcelona.

Editorial Abril. 1976. *El libro del fútbol.* Editorial Abril, Buenos Aires.

Escobar Bavio, Ernesto. 1953. *Alumni, cuna de campeones.* Editorial Difusión, Buenos Aires.

Fabbri, Alejandro. 2008. *Historias negras del fútbol argentino.* Capital Intelectual, Buenos Aires.

Foer, Franklin. 2004. *How Soccer Explains the World.* Harper Collins, New York.

Foot, John. 2007. *Calcio, A History of Italian Football.* Harper Perennial, London.

Fucks, Diego. 2005. *Duelo de guapos.* Distal, Buenos Aires.

Galeano, Eduardo. 1995. *El fútbol a sol y sombra.* Catálogos, Buenos Aires.

Galvis Ramírez, Alberto. 2008. *100 años de fútbol en Colombia.* Planeta, Bogotá.

Goldblatt, David. *The Ball Is Round.* Penguin Books, London.

González, Carlos; Navarrete, Luis; Quezada, Braian. 2014. *La roja.* RIL Editores, Santiago de Chile.

Harvey, Adrian. 2005. *Football, the First Hundred Years. The Untold Story.* Routledge, London.

Hesse-Lichtenberger, Ulrich. 2003. *Tor! The Story of German Football.* WSC Books, London.

Historia del Fútbol Argentino. 1994. Diario La Nación, Buenos Aires.

Historia del Fútbol Argentino. 1955. Editorial Eiffel, Buenos Aires.

Historia El Gráfico de la selección argentina. 1997. El Gráfico, Buenos Aires.

Hofmarcher, Arnaud. 2010. *Carton rouge.* Le cherche midi, Paris.

Inglis, Simon. 1987. *The Football Grounds of Great Britain.* Willow Books, London.

Iucht, Román. 2010. *La vida por el fútbol. Marcelo Bielsa, el último romántico.* Sudamericana, Buenos Aires.

Iwanczuk, Jorge. 1992. *Historia del fútbol amateur en la Argentina.* Jorge Iwanczuk, Buenos Aires.

Kuper, Simon. 2006. *Soccer Against the Enemy.* Nation Books, New York.

Lauduique-Hamez, Sylvie. 2006. *Les incroyables du football.* Calmann-Levy, Paris.

Les miscellanées du foot. 2009. Éditions Solar, Paris.

Litvin, Aníbal. 2013. *1.000 datos locos del fútbol mundial.* V&R Editoras, Buenos Aires.

Lodge, Robert. 2010. *1001 Bizarre Football Stories.* Carlton Books, London.

Lowndes, William. 1964. *The story of Football.* The Sportsmans Book Club, London.

Ludden, John. 2010. *Los partidos del siglo.* TyB Editores, Madrid.

MacWilliam, Rab. 2013. *We Are the Champions.* Endeavour Press, London.

Mármol de Moura, Marcelo. 2014. *Los 200 partidos más curiosos del fútbol argentino.* Corregidor, Buenos Aires.

Mas, Sergi. 2009. *Anécdotas de fútbol.* Libros Cúpula, Barcelona.

Masnou, Albert, et al. 2007. *La pelota nunca se cansa.* Editorial Base, Barcelona.

Matthews, Tony. 2009. *Football Oddities*. The History Press, Stroud.

Murray, Colin. 2010. *A Random History of Football*. Orion Books, London.

Palermo, Martín. 2011. *Titán del gol y de la vida, mi autobiografía*. Planeta, Buenos Aires.

Peredo, Daniel. 2011. *Los 500 datos caletas de la Copa América*. De Chalaca, Lima.

Prats, Luis. 2010. *La crónica celeste*. Fin de Siglo, Montevideo.

Phythian, Graham. 2005. *Colossus*. Tempus Publishing Ltd., Stroud.

Relaño, Alfredo. 2010. *366 historias del fútbol mundial que deberías saber*. Ediciones Martínez Roca, Madrid.

Rey, Alfonso, and Rojas, Pablo. 1947. *El fútbol argentino*. Ediciones Nogal, Buenos Aires.

Rice, Jonathan. 1996. *Curiosities of Football*. Pavilion Books, London.

Risolo, Donn. 2010. *Soccer Stories*. University of Nebraska Press, Lincoln.

Samper Camargo, Nicolás, et al. 2008. *Bestiario del balón*. Aguilar, Bogotá.

Sanders, Richard. 2009. *Beastly Fury, the Strange Birth of British Football*. Bantam Books, London.

Señorans, Jorge. 2014. *Son cosas del fútbol*. Fin de Siglo, Montevideo.

Sharpe, Graham. 2009. *500 Strangest Football Stories*. Racing Post Books, Compton.

Simpson, Paul, and Hesse, Uli. 2014. *Who Invented the Bicycle Kick?* Harper Collins, New York.

Snyder, John. 2001. *Soccer's Most Wanted*. Potomac Books, Virginia.

Southgate, Vera. 2012. *The Story of Football*. Ladybird Books, London.

Tabares, Javier, and Bolaños, Eduardo. 2012. *Esto (también) es fútbol*. Planeta, Buenos Aires.

Talic, Daniel, and De Lucca, Guillermo. 2009. *Diccionario del fútbol*. Claridad, Buenos Aires.

Thomson, Gordon. 1998. *The Man in Black*. Prion Books Limited, London.

Tovar, Jorge. 2014. *Números redondos*. Grijalbo, Bogotá.

Venegas Traverso, Cristián. 2013. *Fuera de juego*. Editorial Forja, Santiago de Chile.

Ward, Andrew. 2002. *Football's Strangest Matches*. Portico, Londres.

Wernicke, Luciano. 1996. *Curiosidades Futboleras*. Editorial Sudamericana, Buenos Aires.

Wernicke, Luciano. 1997. *Curiosidades Futboleras II*. Editorial Sudamericana, Buenos Aires.

Wernicke, Luciano. 2008. *Nuevas curiosidades futboleras*. Ediciones Al Arco, Buenos Aires.

Wernicke, Luciano. 2013. *Historias insólitas del fútbol*. Planeta, Buenos Aires.

Wernicke, Luciano. 2015. *Historias insólitas de la Copa Libertadores*. Planeta, Buenos Aires.

Wernicke, Luciano. 2015. *Curiosidades de la Copa América*. Ediciones Al Arco, Buenos Aires.

Wilson, Jonathan. 2009. *Inverting the Pyramid*. Orion Books, London.

Wilson, Jonathan. 2012. *The Outsider, a History of the Goalkeeper*. Orion Books, London.

Newspapers

Argentina: *Clarín, La Nación, Olé, Diario Popular, Crónica, La Prensa, La Razón, Uno, Libre, Página/12.*

Bolivia: *La Razón.*

Brazil: *O Estado, Lance, Folha de São Paulo.*

Chile: *La Tercera, El Mercurio.*

Colombia: *El Tiempo, El País.*
Ecuador: *Hoy, El Telégrafo.*
France: *Le Dauphiné.*
Italy: *Corriere Della Sera, La Repubblica, La Stampa.*
Paraguay: *ABC Color.*
Perú: *El Comercio, El Nacional.*
Spain: *As, Marca, El Mundo, El País, La Vanguardia, Mundo Deportivo, ABC de Sevilla.*
United Kingdom: *Daily Mail, The Times, Evening Standard, Daily Telegraph, Daily Mirror, The Independent, Herald Scotland, WalesOnLine.*
United States: *New York Times, New York Post, Los Angeles Times, Los Angeles Sentinel.*
Uruguay: *El País, El Observador.*
Venezuela: *El Universal.*

Magazines

Campeón (Argentina)
El Gráfico (Argentina)
Four Four Two (UK)
Guerin Sportivo (Italy)
Mundo deportivo (Argentina)
Placar (Brazil)
Soho (Colombia)
Sports Illustrated (USA)
Total Football (UK)
Un Caño (Argentina)

News Agencies

Diarios y Noticias (Argentina)
Telam (Argentina)

Reuters (UK)
Deutsche Presse Agentur (Alemania)
EFE (Spain)
Agence France Press (France)
Agenzia Nazionale Stampa Associata (Italy)
United Press International (USA)
Associated Press (USA)

Websites

footballsite.co.uk
fifa.com
uefa.com

CREDITS

Design & Layout

Cover & interior design: Annika Naas
Layout: Amnet
Cover image: © AdobeStock

Editorial

Managing editor: Elizabeth Evans
Translator: Hernán Amorini

Trabajo publicado en el marco del Programa de Apoyo a la Traducción "Sur" del Ministerio de Relaciones Exteriores, Comercio Internacional y Culto de la República Argentina.

MORE SOCCER NARRATIVES

240 p., b/w, paperback,
5.5" x 8.5"
ISBN: 978-1-78255-137-9
$14.95 US

Luciano Wernicke

WHY IS SOCCER PLAYED ELEVEN AGAINST ELEVEN?
Everything You Need to Know About Soccer

This book reveals 100 facts of soccer history and rules that are not well known, such as why soccer is played eleven against eleven, why soccer matches last 90 minutes, and who invented goal nets, red and yellow cards, and the penalty shoot-out. Also included are funny and weird anecdotes, making this book the most complete and entertaining resource on the beautiful game of soccer.

FROM
MEYER & MEYER SPORT

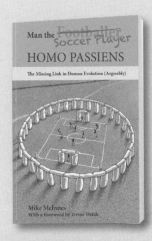
MEYER & MEYER Sport
Von-Coels-Str. 390
52080 Aachen
Germany

Phone   +49 02 41 - 9 58 10 - 13
Fax   +49 02 41 - 9 58 10 - 10
E-Mail sales@m-m-sports.com
E-Books www.m-m-sports.com

All books available as E-books.

MEYER
& MEYER
SPORT

GREAT SOCCER TITLES

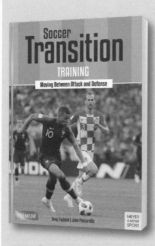

312 p., in color,
212 photos + illus.,
paperback,
6.5" x 9.5"
ISBN: 978-1-78255-151-5
$24.95 US

Englund/Pascarella

SOCCER TRANSITION TRAINING
Moving Between Attack and Defense

The 2018 World Cup highlighted the increasing emphasis on traditional awareness and tactics and the advantages which can be seized by controlling transitional moments during a match. This book offers everything coaches at any level need to help their teams dominate in transition, including transition analysis, comprehensive examination of tactical opportunities, 100 exercises and variations to prepare for every transitional situation, and coaching instruction.

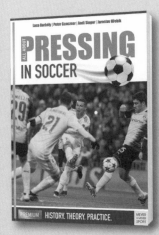